The Vigilant
INVESTOR

*A Former SEC Enforcer Reveals
How to Fraud-Proof Your Investments*

Pat Huddleston

ΛMACOM

American Management Association

New York ✦ Atlanta ✦ Brussels ✦ Chicago ✦ Mexico City ✦ San Francisco
Shanghai ✦ Tokyo ✦ Toronto ✦ Washington, D.C.

Library of Congress Cataloging-in-Publication Data

Huddleston, Pat.
  The vigilant investor : a former SEC enforcer reveals how to fraud-proof your investments / Pat Huddleston.—1st ed.
    p.   cm.
  Includes index.
  ISBN-13: 978-0-8144-1750-8
  ISBN-10: 0-8144-1750-7
  1. Investments.   2. Securities fraud.   3. Swindlers and swindling—Prevention.   I. Title.
HG4521.H846   2011
332.6—dc23

                                                                    2011019827

About AMA
American Management Association (www.amanet.org) is a world leader in talent development, advancing the skills of individuals to drive business success. Our mission is to support the goals of individuals and organizations through a complete range of products and services, including classroom and virtual seminars, webcasts, webinars, podcasts, conferences, corporate and government solutions, business books, and research. AMA's approach to improving performance combines experiential learning—learning through doing—with opportunities for ongoing professional growth at every step of one's career journey.

Printing number

10   9   8   7   6   5   4   3   2   1

Contents

Acknowledgments

I describe in the Introduction the moment that the idea for an investor protection company came to me. All I've done since is to follow where that idea led. All credit for the good we've done and that this book will do belongs to God. He's blessed our efforts mostly through the people he's put in our path; people like Wendy Keller, my literary agent, and Bob Nirkind, my editor at AMACOM, both of whom were, by turns, gracious and firm with this rookie author. At Investor's Watchdog, Lauren Bowman and Rosey Sumrall have been diligent fact checkers, as has Cherie Eason, my senior legal assistant and right arm in law practice. I am forever indebted to my former colleagues in the Atlanta office of the SEC. They made me a fraud hunter and infused a spirit of public service that stuck when I returned to private law practice. My brothers and sisters at North Metro Church have been a constant source of encouragement. It is a long path to publication, and I'd never have been able to envision the end clearly enough to begin the journey without lessons in possibility, determination, and hard work from my parents, Mike and Bettie, and unwavering love and support from my brothers, Porter and Matthew. Porter, the true writer in the family, gave invaluable guidance over the many months that we worked to find an agent and craft a winning proposal. All love and thanks to my wife Carol, our family MVP, who bore the strain of the effort with grace while giving our sons, Mike and Ben, love, support, and guidance. Finally, thanks to every victim of investment fraud who is brave enough to throw off misplaced guilt and shame to seek justice.

*To the memory of
Bettie Beck Huddleston,
my loving Mom.
All glory to God.*

Introduction

In July 2006, I closed the door of my law office after saying good-bye to a 70-year-old man who had lost his life savings to a Ponzi scheme. This retiree—a family patriarch who had saved for decades in hopes of paying for his grandchildren's college educations—had come to me because he knew that I had been an Enforcement Branch Chief at the U.S. Securities and Exchange Commission (SEC). He wanted me to help him get his nest egg back, but I couldn't. The confidence man who had taken it had no liability insurance, and he had never worked for a brokerage firm that could have detected and prevented the scam. The con man had spent this senior citizen's nest egg, and many others', on homes, cars, expensive vacations, and phony "distribution" payments to earlier investors. I could have won this prospective client a multimillion-dollar civil judgment—including punitive damages and attorney's fees—but we would never have collected a dime.

In more than two decades of protecting investors, both as an SEC enforcer and as an attorney for investors, I'd had conversations like this one with hundreds of investors, from institutions to blue-collar retirees. It's never fun, especially with seniors, who cannot rebuild their nest eggs through several more decades of work. Usually they try to remain stoic, but you can see them deflate and their minds wander to the painful practical implications of the bad news. The blood drains from their faces as they try to reconcile their image of themselves as smart and competent with the reality that a stranger has already spent the money that it took them decades to earn and save. Sometimes they shed tears of shame and humiliation, feeling more guilt in that moment than the people who defrauded them will feel in their entire lives.

I expected nothing more from the rest of the afternoon than I'd experienced all of the other times I'd given this kind of bad news: a lingering sadness. But this day was different. As I turned away from the door, a thought exploded into my head with lightning-strike power; I actually felt a physical impact. *How long are you going to keep having these conversations before you do something to protect these people?* In that moment, Investor's Watchdog, LLC, was born.

We began by building a database to hold information on stockbrokers, investment advisers, and scam artists nationwide. We added thousands of customer complaints that had been expunged from stockbrokers' official regulatory rap sheets—not because the brokers were exonerated, but because the brokers made this a condition of settlement with their victims. We gathered information on actions against the horde of unregistered salespeople who operate off the regulatory grid. We put it all in the IW database.

Within days of launching Investor's Watchdog, we saved a church in Arizona from losing its entire building fund to a con man who was operating under an assumed name. Since 2006, Investor's Watchdog has investigated unregistered investments on three continents, including supposed luxury resorts on the Red Sea; investments in renovated hotels in the United Kingdom; private banks in Geneva, Switzerland; and oil and gas projects in Texas. We've also investigated stockbrokers that the Financial Industry Regulatory Authority (FINRA) rates as perfectly clean but who have been the subject of so many customer complaints that no investor would ever use them if he knew the truth.

Shortly after opening Investor's Watchdog, I received my first assignment as a court-appointed receiver in an SEC fraud case, cleaning up the mess from the collapse of an investment scam in South

Carolina. I've cleaned up that kind of mess in three SEC cases as of this writing (one involving an international hedge fund fraud), and two more for the Federal Trade Commission. That work has taken me all over the United States and beyond, closing down fraudulent operations, recovering assets from overseas, and pursuing litigation (against people who received investors' funds or who contributed to the scam) to generate a fund from which to repay investors. Sometimes we've been able to pay back more than half of what was lost. Other times, we've been able to return only nickels on the dollar. Although our receivership work always produces far more for investors than it costs, we cannot make the victims whole. We can neither unscramble their nest eggs nor fully assuage the feelings of humiliation and misplaced guilt that grip them in the wake of their financial loss.

In 2008, hoping to reach more investors, I launched www.invest orswatchblog.com, where we cover the hundreds of financial scams that come to light every year. I write a new post every weekday, linking to a news story about the case and drawing lessons from it that can help others avoid a similar fate. Most days I have to choose from among several scams that have come to light in the previous 24 hours.

The FBI estimates that Americans lose $40 billion annually to investment fraud. That's the equivalent of one Madoff-sized megafraud every single year. And the problem is only getting worse. Despite access to innumerable resources published by regulators and consumer reporters on how to avoid scams, we are falling for them in record numbers. Why? There are three reasons. First, the pool of attractive victims is bigger. If there was ever a time to get into the investment fraud business, this is it. The first baby boomers began turning 65 in May 2011 and will turn 65 at the rate of 10,000 per day until 2030. As they retire, those boomers will move $2.5 trillion in assets from the relative safety of company-sponsored 401(k) accounts into self-directed accounts at brokerage firms, where they will be as vulnerable as a wounded rabbit in the forest.

Second, the world is getting smaller. Technology allows con men in Russia and Dubai to rob pension plans, business owners, baby boomers, and senior citizens in America, while American scamsters can return the favor, swindling investors wherever people speak English.

Finally, the advice we get from regulators and well-meaning consumer reporters is always dangerously incomplete. It fails to address key information that is emerging from those who study the science of decision making. That information explains why, despite all the warnings, we are so prone to fall victim to investment fraud and unethical brokers.

Contrary to almost universal belief, neither gullibility nor low intelligence is the problem. U.S. presidents, rocket scientists, Ph.D.s, MBAs, CPAs, FBI special agents, lawyers, experts on gullibility, and more members of the American Medical Association than you could fit in the nearest major league stadium have been victimized by investment fraud. The real culprit behind the worsening epidemic is the human brain—specifically, the cognitive biases that come as default settings in every healthy mind. While they are helpful in other contexts, those biases skew how we view information in the investment context, leading us to trust people who have every intention of breaching that trust and leading us into shallow inquiries that we mistake for in-depth investigations. An investor who memorizes a complete list of helpful "dos and don'ts" without first appreciating the power of cognitive biases is like an NHL All-Star without his skates; he has impressive knowledge and talent without having the ability to put it to practical use.

And it isn't only individual investors who fall victim to scamsters. Underfunded pension plans, desperate for a rate of return that will bring them back into the black, fall prey to world-class con artists, as do endowments, school districts, and family offices. People who make decisions for institutional investors are more popular with scam artists than sweet tea at a barbecue.

The securities industry is as dirty as a plumber's boots. Multimillion-dollar advertising budgets and the charisma and salesmanship of individual brokers keep most investors in an anesthetic fog, through which they cannot perceive a landscape that is strewn with mines and traps. *The Vigilant Investor* burns away that fog. We'll tour an industry that is indifferent, at best, to the welfare of investors. This journey will equip you to protect yourself from characters who are determined to take as much of your money for themselves as possible.

Sir Arthur Conan Doyle understood that the ability to uncover carefully crafted and expertly concealed misconduct has everything to do with experience. In *A Study in Scarlet*, Sherlock Holmes explains, "There is a strong family resemblance about misdeeds, and *if you have all the details of a thousand at your finger ends*, it is odd if you cannot unravel the thousand and first." What investors lack, and what they desperately need, are the details of the thousand misdeeds to which Holmes refers. This book puts the details of many misdeeds at your finger ends to better enable you to unravel the many scams and unethical advisers that will target you over a lifetime of investing.

Because experience is the best teacher, those who have seen hundreds of scams and reckless brokers are best equipped to uncover a well-disguised ongoing scam or a broker who intends to feast on your savings. I've spoken to every type of investment criminal imaginable, from professional con artists to fund managers who began with good intentions, from highly functioning sociopaths to ineffectual bunglers, from those who flee the country when the jig is up to those who attempt to fake their own death. I've seen scams and unethical financial advisers up close from a unique combination of perspectives: SEC enforcer, court-appointed receiver, attorney for investors, blogger on breaking scams, and founder and CEO of a professional due diligence company. I know how scams and unethical advisers begin, how they operate, what contributes to their longevity, and what tactics they use to ensnare individual and institutional investors alike. I know how to recognize scams and bad advisers that other investigators miss. This book is my way of equipping you to do likewise.

We've organized the book in two parts. Part 1 explores the wide world of investment fraud. It begins with an examination of cognitive biases and explains how to defuse them. We then look at several categories of scam artist, some of their favorite con games, and the advanced tactics that they use to pull off these games. Along the way, we give you advice that will protect you from getting conned. We close Part 1 with a look into the future of investment fraud, where scams will be bigger, last longer, and be harder to spot.

Part 2 narrows the focus to the U.S. securities industry. We begin by introducing the investment cops and the limits of their power. We then perform a harsh light-of-day examination of the usual suspects (stockbrokers, registered investment advisers, and insurance agents), the duties they owe to investors, and how they often use investors as tools for their own enrichment. We also look at brokers who target the most vulnerable of investors, the elderly, and provide advice on how adult children can protect their elderly parents. We close the book with a vision of how vigilant investors can band together to cleanse the investing landscape as no investment cop ever can.

Each chapter uses actual examples of scamsters and brokers who swindled very bright, but not-yet-vigilant, investors. We provide guidance on how a vigilant investor should approach an investigation of those scams. We conclude each chapter with a section entitled "Due Diligence for the Vigilant," which sums up, in bulleted list form, the action items that will keep the vigilant investor clear of the characters and tricks that have cost so many so much.

As hard as they work and as dedicated as they are, regulators cannot keep you safe. Because it has more lobbying dollars than investors can ever contribute, the securities industry has been—and will always be—successful in keeping the investment cops severely understaffed and underfunded. Even causing a once-in-a-century financial crisis has not diminished the securities industry's influence. The successful solution, therefore, to an epidemic that will rob institutional investors, baby boomers, and the elderly of more than $1 trillion over the coming generation cannot involve Congress and must be immune to the influence of lobbyists.

Where can we find such a solution? In your mirror. Using the tools you'll find in here, you can do what no Congress or investment cop ever will. You can close down professional scams before they get off the ground. You can run unethical brokers out of the business. You can protect not only yourself and those you love, but countless others.

There is a path through the well-disguised traps and pitfalls that litter the investing landscape to a retirement full of the blessings that hard work and savings make possible. This book maps that path for all who are wise enough to follow it. Let's go.

The Wide World of Fraud

*First Steps and Advanced Tactics
on the Path to Vigilant Investing*

1

Vigilant or Vigilante?

Protecting Your Investments in the Age of Fraud

Know thyself

—THE ORACLE AT DELPHI

He who trusts himself is a fool, but he
who walks in wisdom keeps safe.

—PROVERBS 28:26

Roland Koenig is 76 years old. He lives in Traunstein, Germany. Roland's wife, Sieglinde, is 81. She does not live with Roland, but she visits him as often as her arthritis allows.

Roland is in prison. If he survives his prison stretch, he will walk free in 2015 at the age of 81. When he earns time in the prison yard, Roland gets to see his friend Willy Dehmer, who entered prison with him a year and a half ago. Their path to prison made international news, and their story resonates with the millions of investors who fall victim to financial scams every year.

11

The Federal Bureau of Investigation (FBI) says that Americans lose $40 billion to investment fraud each year. My experience tells me that the total is much higher than that and that American losses are only a small fraction of the worldwide totals.

Despite our unprecedented access to information, the problem is only getting worse—much worse. Something is happening that access to more information by itself cannot cure. We will discover what that something is and learn how we can make ourselves, and those who count on us, safer by adding—of all things—an accurate mirror to our investment toolbox.

The Geritol Gang

In the early 1990s, the Koenigs, Dehmer, and their friends Gerald and Iris Fell traveled from their homes in Germany to vacation together in Naples, Florida. That's where they met investment adviser Jim Amburn and learned how much they had in common with him.

The son of a German mother and an American G.I., Amburn was born in Germany and lived there until he was 10, when he moved to the United States. He studied economics in college and worked on Wall Street for a decade before moving to Florida to open an investment advisory business called Digital Global Net USA, Inc. Amburn still had a home in Speyer, Germany, near the southwestern border with France.

A friendship blossomed. In 1997, when the Koenigs decided to buy a vacation home in Aventura, Florida, Amburn helped them buy it. When the Koenigs and their friends traveled there, Amburn made the two-hour drive across Alligator Alley to pay them a visit. It seemed only natural that they would say yes when Amburn proposed helping them invest their retirement savings.

According to testimony in the trial that sent Roland Koenig to prison, Amburn told the Koenigs and their friends that he could earn them 18 percent per year through a "money fund" tied to the real estate market. They believed him and handed over a total of $3.2 million.

At first, the German retirees were pleased with Amburn's management. The interest checks from Amburn arrived right on time . . . until they didn't. Amburn ultimately told his German friends that all of their money had been lost, a casualty of the subprime mortgage collapse.

In the summer of 2008, Amburn was staying at his home in Speyer. Returning from the local pub one day, he walked into an ambush at his front door. Roland Koenig and his friends were there. They talked their way into Amburn's house by saying that they wanted to discuss their investments. Perhaps hoping to pacify the group, Amburn invited them in. At Roland's signal, the group attacked Amburn, knocked him down, and beat him with their walkers. The senior citizens used duct tape to bind Amburn, stopping several times to catch their breath. When they were finished, Amburn looked mummified and was certain that he was destined for the fate of the pharaohs.

The Geritol Gang, as the press called them, consisted of Roland; Sieglinde; Willy Dehmer (61 years old); Gerald Fell (68 years old); and his wife, Iris (64 years old). The gang put Amburn in a box that Roland had built for the occasion. They used a hand truck to wheel Amburn to an Audi 8 sedan, loaded him into the trunk, and began a 300-mile trek to the Koenigs' home on the shores of Lake Chiemsee in Bavaria. The gang stopped for gas once and opened the box, perhaps to make sure that their captive was still alive. Amburn, who had worked himself partially loose from his bonds, attempted to escape, earning himself a beating that broke two of his ribs. The gang stuffed him back into the box and continued the journey.

What awaited Amburn at the house on the lake gave him little hope that he would survive the ordeal. In the basement of the house were a metal cot, to which he was chained, and a portable toilet. According to Amburn's testimony at the trial, the gang burned him with cigarettes, beat him with a chair leg, and threatened him with a visit from the Russian mafia, all the while demanding that he return the money that they had entrusted to him. He repeated his claim that it had all been lost in the subprime crash. The gang did not believe him.

After more than two days in the dungeon, Amburn hatched a plan. He told the gang that he could wire money from a Swiss bank to their accounts if they would give him access to a fax machine. The gang told Amburn to write out the instructions for the wire transfers, which he did. He then added the plea "CALL POLICE" in the written instructions. Whether because of their bad eyesight or the spelling of the German word for *policy* (p-o-l-i-c-e), the kidnappers did not notice Amburn's ploy. They faxed the phony instructions to Credit Suisse. Amburn had no money there, but he prayed that someone would see his message. Someone did.

Convinced that their captive had finally seen the futility of denying that he could return their money, the gang allowed him a smoke break in the walled-in courtyard behind the house. A thunderstorm was brewing as Amburn, stripped to his underpants, smoked a cigarette and worried that no one at the bank would notice his plea for help. As the storm broke, dropping a curtain of rain between him and the elderly sentinels watching him from inside the house, Amburn's desperation overtook him. He gathered his remaining strength and scrambled over the brick wall. He made his way to the road in front of the house and began running toward town, screaming as he went.

Realizing that they could not catch a 57-year-old with several yards' head start—walkers being good for balance and for bludgeoning investment advisers, but a serious hindrance to speed—the gang piled into the Audi and pursued Amburn up the road, yelling out the windows that they had caught the man burglarizing their home. A pair of neighbors knocked him down and pinned him to the road until the gang could bind him again and stuff him back into the car. Amburn testified at the trial that the escape attempt earned him another beating when the gang got him back to the makeshift dungeon.

Tipped off by bankers at Credit Suisse, 40 German police officers in commando gear descended on the house and freed Amburn, then had to call a doctor to help the gang members into police vans because of their various infirmities. Amburn's ordeal had lasted four days.

A judge in Traunstein, Bavaria, sentenced Roland to six years in prison. Willy Dehmer received four years. Sieglinde got 21 months, and Iris Fell 18 months, but the judge suspended their sentences. Gerald Fell was too ill to stand trial. He will be tried later if he ever recovers.

As of this writing, Amburn is under investigation. Whether he considers that investigation more humiliating than having his can kicked by slow-moving, arthritic senior citizens, one of whom had exceeded her actuarial life span, only he can say.

Unless you have lost your life savings to fraud or to a reckless or incompetent financial adviser, you cannot appreciate the desperation that grips people who learn that the product of their hard work and diligent saving is suddenly gone. Having spoken to hundreds of such people, I can tell you that it is the rare person among them who does not at least consider extracting vigilante justice from the individual who caused the loss. The reversal of financial fortunes hits like a physical impact, like a spine-splintering highway collision that alters the trajectory of one or more lives.

Among the tragedies wrapped up in the wreckage is that the collision was avoidable. Although victims sometimes console themselves with the idea that their situation was "the perfect storm," that there was nothing that they could have done differently to avoid the scam, such is not the case.

To be fair to those investors, avoiding these life-altering financial collisions is not nearly as easy as those who view it from the sidelines think as they comfort themselves with the thought, "I'd never have fallen for that." The truth is that almost every human being in identical circumstances would have fallen for it. Believing otherwise is an invitation to be proven wrong in a devastating and humiliating fashion.

As the story of the Geritol Gang illustrates, attempts at vigilante justice always end badly. What works instead is preinvestment vigilance. And that vigilance must begin with an understanding of the psychological and neurological factors—common to all healthy humans—that make us all so susceptible to losing our nest eggs. Until we understand that scam victims are *not* a genetically deficient subset of extraordinarily gullible and/or greedy rubes, we cannot become the vigilant investors who reap the benefits of hard work and careful saving and pass wealth on to the next generation.

"That Could Never Happen to Me"

Imagine that you open the newspaper, or your favorite news web site, this morning and read that a group of 300 senior citizens in Nebraska have lost a total of $100 million to a phony certificate of deposit scam. You read the details about the scam operator's lavish lifestyle and previous run-ins with securities regulators in Iowa, Kansas, and South Dakota; about the 10 percent rate of return that he guaranteed; and about how he prepared phony account statements to lull his victims into believing that their money was safe and sound. What would be your initial reactions to that story? Write them down.

Now check the list. Somewhere on that list is a reaction that blames the victims. You might not come right out and call them "gullible," "stupid," or "greedy," but you have at least some sense that through their negligence the victims were contributors to their own financial ruin. We see the same phenomenon when we read about a tragedy involving a child. Among our first reactions is, "Where were the parents?" Is that not so?

Do you see what is happening? Very quickly, we begin to focus on the victims and what they did or failed to do that contributed to their downfall. Give yourself some credit; the questions about what the victims could have done to protect their nest eggs are valid. Answering those questions is what this book is about. But what I want you to notice is how quickly the thought occurs to you. Why is that?

We have a hardwired defensive reaction to stories about tragedy. Our minds automatically work to distance us from the victims as a way of protecting us from the painful contemplation of what it would be like to be in the victims' shoes. We hate feeling vulnerable. So we mentally distinguish ourselves from the group that is feeling the pain of the tragedy. The unspoken subtitle to "I'd never have fallen for that" or "Where were the parents?" is, "That could never happen to me."

"Too Smart to Fall for It"

Another unspoken reaction to learning of the tragedy of a stolen nest egg is, "I'm too smart to fall for that." Those with higher education, white-collar jobs, substantial wealth, and/or investment experience are especially prone to that very dangerous thought.

Before they invested with Bernard Madoff, the people whom he preyed upon had lost more money in their collective couch cushions than I will make in the next two years. They were high achievers who had combined intelligence, education, and hard work to provide themselves with very comfortable circumstances. Before they met Bernie Madoff, they would have judged themselves the least likely people in the world to lose money to an investment fraud. And yet, many of them lost everything.

So impressive were Madoff's victims that, if you could move past your visceral reaction to Madoff, you might even be tempted to feel a kind of disgusted admiration for his ability to pluck such difficult pigeons. *How persuasive must he have been to convince people who were that smart—corporate titans and advisers to America's wealthiest people—to invest with him?* Those of us in the investor protection business, though, know that Madoff's "sophisticated" victims were actually low-hanging fruit, easy prey, the $100 question on *Who Wants to Be a Millionaire?*

In my time at the U.S. Securities and Exchange Commission (SEC) in Atlanta, we used to say that if you found an investment that more than two medical doctors had invested in, it was *definitely* a scam—they fall for scams that often. We worked on a case in which an astronaut—literally a rocket scientist—lost hundreds of thousands of dollars. And, if you gathered together all the Ph.D.s, MBAs, DDSs, CPAs, attorneys, and other college graduates we talked to who had lost six figures to a scam, you could not stuff them all into Ted Turner's biggest house.

What is it about successful, well-educated people, then, that leads them to fall for investment scams at least as often as the average Joe? No doubt, scam artists target them more often, because, as Willie Sutton said, "That's where the money is." But, even adjusting for income, well-educated, financially savvy investors fall for scams more often than those with less financial knowledge.

Pride Goeth Before . . .

The problem is our pride—not the kind of pride we are expressing when we tell a family member or friend, "I am proud of you," nor the kind we feel at hailing from a particular country, state, school, or team. The kind of pride we mean is the kind we describe down south as "putting on airs," the kind that makes us feel puffed up with the thought that we are smarter, better looking, more insightful, and so on than the next guy, and that makes us hate to admit that we are wrong.

To be sure, self-confidence is important to success. No one who walks around convinced that he is an idiot will go very far. But there is an imperceptible line between self-confidence, which is healthy, and hubris (overbearing pride or presumption), which is deadly. The gravitational pull on the hubris side of that line is strong. The closer we come to it, the less likely we are to resist its pull. The scam artist's modus operandi always includes pushing prospective marks[1] closer to that line.

The pride attack is subtle and effective, but it requires very little work on the part of the scam artist; the mark does all of the heavy lifting. Whether the amount of the investment is $1 million or $10,000, the scam artist will feign an assumption that you have the education and experience to know the definition of all the terms she uses and to understand how all the moving parts of the investment work together to generate an attractive return. The scamster knows that, being human, you will not want to make any statement that might be translated as, "I am not that smart," especially when you think you ought to know what the communicator is talking about.

This is especially true for financially successful people. Their income buys them a very nice lifestyle, and they often feel pressure—driven by a need to maintain their image of competence—to feign an understanding of every section of the *Wall Street Journal.* Of course, making money often has nothing to do with understanding the finer points of economics and the ins and outs of the world's capital and debt markets. But financially successful people often believe that they should know those things, and they hate admitting that they don't.

No advice on avoiding fraud, not even, "Never invest in anything you don't understand," will ever do us any good until we understand how pride makes it hard to follow that advice. Presidents, astronauts, rocket scientists, Ph.D.s, MBAs, and probably more than half the members of the American Medical Association have been victimized by scam artists. The vigilant investor understands that his education, list of accomplishments, well-deserved reputation, zip code, bank balance, and press clippings provide no protection; instead, they only make the scam artist's job easier.

But pride is no less dangerous for those without a college degree. You might think that blue-collar workers would feel less pressure to fake an understanding of the complicated terms that a supposed investment professional uses, but all humans, regardless of their training or education, read about scam victims and think, "I'd never fall for that." That thought, all by itself, makes the blue-collar retiree as vulnerable as the guy with more degrees than a thermometer.

Before you breathe a sigh of relief at the thought that you are not a prideful person, consider that C. S. Lewis described pride as "the one vice of which no man is free."[2] English author and lexicographer Samuel Johnson would have agreed. He wrote, "Pride is a vice, which pride itself inclines every man to find in others, and overlook in himself."[3] If you were as humble as Mother Teresa, you would still have enough pride for a scam artist to fan into a blaze that would consume your nest egg unless you smothered it with an understanding of your nature and the scam artist's manipulations.

Part of the reason that we are not better at defending ourselves against appeals to our pride is that we have bad information about the consequences of that pride. If you ask most people for a quotation about pride, they will repeat the old axiom, "Pride goeth before a fall." But how helpful is that? What disaster has it saved you from lately?

We understand what harmful "pride" is, but "fall" is a broad term. From what height do we make this metaphorical fall? How hard do we fall? Into what? The axiom lacks punch as a warning against pride. Perhaps that is because it is a misstatement of a real, and much more powerful, proverb from the Bible. Proverbs 16:18 reads, "Pride goes before *destruction* and a haughty spirit before a fall." Now *that* is a statement of helpful truth, especially in the investment context. "Destruction" we understand. Think Hiroshima.

Humans Being Human: What Psychiatrists and Neuroscientists Tell Us About Ourselves

Twenty years of protecting investors have taught me that hardwired defense mechanisms and pride combine to convince us that victims of investment fraud are just plain country-come-to-town gullible; that they are future nominees for a Darwin Award; that they cannot tell you who is buried in Grant's tomb; and that they would look up if you said, "Look, a dead bird." But that is not the case.

Professor Stephen Greenspan can tell us something about gullibility. He wrote the book on it, literally. Published in December 2008, just days after Bernie Madoff turned himself in, *The Annals of Gullibility: Why We Get Duped and How to Avoid It*[4] sold well.

Professor Greenspan knows what he is talking about. He has degrees from Johns Hopkins and Northwestern. He has his Ph.D. in developmental psychology. He is on the faculty at both the University of Connecticut and the University of Colorado. He is a brilliant man. He is also on the long list of Bernard Madoff's victims.

To be fair to Professor Greenspan, he is on that list because the investment adviser to whom he entrusted his nest egg sent it to Madoff. Professor Greenspan nevertheless fell for his investment adviser's promise that the nest egg was invested wisely with Madoff.

I hope we agree that if the guy who wrote the book on gullibility fell for an investment scam, there must be something else going on here besides gullibility as we typically understand it. Indeed, something else *is* going on. Scientists tell us that what's happening is a virulent outbreak of humans being human.

In March 2005, Kristen J. Prentice, Ph.D., James M. Gold, Ph.D., and William T. Carpenter Jr., M.D., published a paper called "Optimistic Bias in the Perception of Personal Risk: Patterns in Schizophrenia" in the *American Journal of Psychiatry*. On their way to drawing conclusions about optimism in schizophrenics, they first discussed optimism in healthy adults. What they found gave a scientific explanation for something that I had observed, but had been unable to explain, for 20 years:

> Risk perception research in healthy adults shows that . . . they frequently exhibit a bias known as "unrealistic optimism" in which individuals feel they are less likely than other people to experience unpleasant or harmful events in their lives but more likely to experience pleasant or beneficial events.[5]

Stated another way, people rarely believe that a disaster scenario—including the disaster of financial fraud—can happen to them.

You can understand how this *optimism bias* might be necessary for life in a dangerous world. Even the most pessimistic among us is optimistic enough to leave the house each day and walk into a world of crime and seemingly random disasters. How would we ever be able to do that without a deeply ingrained belief that everything is going to be all right—that even in a world in which so many bad things happen those things are never going to happen to us?

But, as helpful as it is, this optimism bias makes us vulnerable when it comes to our investments. It leads us into a dangerous world without the defenses necessary to protect ourselves.

Think of it this way: When the optimism bias sends us out the front door into a world of crime, germs, and teenage drivers, we have defenses against those. We avoid high-crime areas. Our immune system handles the germs without our even having to think about it. And a few years behind the wheel teaches us that it is highly likely that a teenager is going to run the red light at the next intersection, so we check right and left before we get there, even though we've got the green light.

Unfortunately, we are not born with the defenses necessary to protect our nest eggs. Nevertheless, we have to make a decision about what to do with our retirement savings and/or our college fund. When we venture out to look into our options, we soon find that all roads lead to the same destination.

Whether we enter it through a bank, through a stockbroker or an insurance agent, or through an investment we hear about from our brother-in-law, our search for investment options always takes us into a very impressive metaphorical neighborhood called the *securities industry*. The homes there vary from quaint-looking bungalows to multiacre estates. Most of us feel a bit like Jed Clampett as we drive past the guarded gatehouse (only later will we be able to make sense of the guard's curious expression—*was there a warning in that smile?*). There is a golf course there, a beautiful Georgian clubhouse, an Olympic-sized swimming pool, and even horse stables, a paddock, and a ring where Daddy's little girls take English riding lessons. None of the people there look dangerous. They are all well dressed, drive nice cars, and keep their lawns manicured. Their kids look like they walked out of an ad for The Gap.

While we might feel out of place in this neighborhood, none of our innate defenses rise up to warn us of any danger. In fact, our optimism bias tells us that nothing very bad could happen to us here. But the vigilant investor knows that you are more likely to lose your wallet—your entire nest egg—in this neighborhood than in downtown Atlanta at 2 a.m.

You might be tempted to think that cognitive biases (of which the optimism bias is only one) afflict others, but not you. That's the optimism bias at work; see how sneaky these things are? But advances in brain-imaging technology have proven that they are objective neurochemical events that occur in all healthy people. Let's look at another.

Vasily Klucharev is a neuroscientist and a research fellow at Erasmus University in Rotterdam, Netherlands. Klucharev created a scientific study in which he asked participants to rate faces for physical beauty on a scale from 1 to 8. The researchers then told some of the participants that their score was higher than the average score, some that it was lower than the average, and some that it was the same.

After distracting the participants by talking about another subject, the researchers suddenly asked each participant to give her ratings again. Most changed their ratings to move closer to the "average."

The researchers performed this study while the participants were connected to a brain-imaging device. What the researchers found was that when people hold an opinion differing from that of others in a group their brains produce an error signal. Our brains are tuned to what other people think about us, and therefore deviation from the group registers as a punishment. Our brain tends to pull us into conformity with the majority opinion, even when all the objective evidence shows that the majority is wrong.

This *conformity bias* plays itself out in the investment context when you believe that others have invested in something and are making money from it. When your colleagues or friends are all making a killing in a limited partnership investment or with a particular stockbroker or investment adviser, and you have a chance to invest, your very human—not gullible—brain will pull you toward conformity with that group.

The good news is that neuroscientists and psychiatrists tell us only about our tendencies. Cognitive biases lose their power once we drag them out into the light and examine them. By understanding cognitive biases, the constant pull of pride, and that the securities industry is much more dangerous than it appears to be, the vigilant investor lays a firm foundation on which to build more advanced defenses to the life-altering financial collision.

The Vigilant Investor and the NFL Quarterback

Jonah Lehrer's book *How We Decide* is a fascinating and highly readable exploration of the human mind.[6] Lehrer uses Tom Brady, the quarterback for the New England Patriots of the National Football League, to illustrate how our emotions—contrary to popular understanding—are essential to sound decision making. He explains that after the ball is snapped Brady has (at most) four seconds to throw the football before a defensive end delivers a possibly career-ending blow to Brady's body. Each of his possible receivers is moving away from him at top speed, followed closely by one (or more) of the best athletes in the world, who is determined to keep the receiver from catching a pass. Each receiver is running in a different pattern to a different part of the field. Some of them are only 10 yards away; some of them are 40 yards or more downfield. Depending on where the defender is, Brady's target might be the receiver's shoe tops, his jersey number, or his outside shoulder. As if that were not enough, Brady must throw the ball not to where the receiver is, but to where he is *going to be* after the time it takes the ball to cover the distance. He must consider all of this while six-and-a-half-foot-tall defensive linemen extend their Sasquatch-sized hands upward to block his vision and, if possible, the ball.

There is not nearly enough time for Brady to consciously consider each of his choices. What leads him to release the ball to the correct receiver is a feeling rather than a thought. He gets a bad feeling when he looks at the first two receivers, and a flood of positive emotion when he sees the third option, the wide receiver, breaking into the area between the linebackers and the safety. His brain has extracted information and relayed a reliable emotion as a kind of immediate *Reader's Digest* summary that Brady relies on in making his decision. Touchdown.

Of course, Brady's emotions in the moment are informed by hours of film study, thousands of practice repetitions, and the memories of every snap he has ever taken in the NFL. Most significantly, his emotions are informed by the 103 interceptions and 1,714 incomplete passes he has thrown. Every one of those "failure" experiences is stored in Brady's brain and helps to determine whether a negative or a positive emotion comes forth to help him decide which receiver to throw to. Those experiences have led him to three Super Bowl victories; two Super Bowl MVP Awards; 261 career touchdowns; and a career quarterback rating of 95.2, higher than that of any other active quarterback with 10 years in the league.

With Brady's experience in mind, let's look at Tim B. Lever, a fictional investor who must decide whether he will invest his nest egg with fictional investment adviser Dennis Golden. Tim lives next door to Chris Wager. Last week at the neighborhood pool, Chris told Tim about an investment through Golden that is paying Chris 12 percent per year, with monthly profit checks arriving right on time. At Chris's suggestion, the three men play a round of golf together. At the end of the round, Tim accepts Golden's invitation to meet at Golden's office to discuss the investment, which Golden describes as a limited partnership opportunity. What neither Chris nor Tim knows yet is that Dennis Golden is running a cleverly disguised Ponzi scheme, and that the monthly profit check that Chris Wager receives next month will probably come from the portion of Tim's nest egg that Tim turns over to Golden this month.

Tim takes in all of the information that Golden gives him. Tim learned on the golf course that Golden graduated from Columbia with a degree in economics, that he worked for Merrill Lynch before leaving to open his own investment advisory firm, and that he launched the investment limited partnership in which he is currently selling interests six months ago. Golden says that his securities attorney works for the most prestigious law firm in Atlanta and used to work for the SEC. Tim learns that the auditor for Golden's firm is one of the big four accounting firms.

Golden gives Tim a thick document called a private placement memorandum (PPM) and a stack of documents that Tim needs to sign and return along with his check for $100,000 (the minimum investment allowed). Tim happens to have that much in a self-directed IRA that he funded with his 401(k) balance from a previous employer.

At home that evening, Tim and his wife, Michelle, look through the PPM. It is full of cautionary language warning that the investment is illiquid (hard to turn into cash) and that it involves a great deal of risk. Worried by that language, and never having seen a PPM before, Tim calls Chris Wager, who has more experience with investments like this.

"Listen," Chris says, "that language is in every single PPM ever written. It is legal CYA language. All I can tell you is that this thing has paid off like clockwork. It's paying our tuition for the kids, and there's still a bit left over every month."

Although Tim certainly has more time to consider the investment than Tom Brady has to consider his receivers, the decision-making process is not all that different. Tim's brain will send up emotions that are informed by his experiences. He enjoyed his day on the golf course with Golden. Columbia is an Ivy League school. The law and accounting firms advising Golden are reputable. Everyone has heard of Merrill Lynch. Golden is licensed by the SEC as an investment adviser. Golden drove a late-model midlife-crisis Corvette to the golf course and had a nearly new set of graphite irons that helped him score just a stroke behind Tim. The details of how the profits are generated, through currency trading, are less clear to Tim, but he figures that a guy with an economics degree from Columbia must understand those things.

Tim decides to throw his nest egg to Dennis Golden. Golden catches the pass and runs all the way out of the stadium with savings that took Tim 15 years to accumulate. Golden leaves the country six weeks later. No one is at his office when the SEC examiners respond to Tim's complaint that the checks have not arrived as promised.

How did Tim's brain lead him astray? In addition to the optimism and conformity biases we've covered so far, Tim fell victim to another cognitive bias that we call the *congruence bias*. The congruence bias leads us to try to confirm our first hypothesis for a given set of facts, and to ignore possible alternative theories that might also explain the facts. In Tim's predicament, the congruence bias led him to seek to confirm his first theory: that the investment offered by Golden was legitimate. He found evidence to confirm that theory in the positive recommendation from Chris Wager, in the professional and successful image that Golden presented, and in Golden's credentials and lifestyle.

Tim ignored the alternative hypothesis: that Golden was producing the apparent returns by making Ponzi-type payments (using the principal invested by later investors to make payments of supposed profits to earlier investors). Had he tried to confirm *that* hypothesis, Tim would have found the evidence to confirm it (we will discuss how in later chapters). Certainly, nothing that Tim learned from Chris or Golden was inconsistent with the Ponzi hypothesis. The congruence bias simply led Tim to consider only one theory.

Like many people who perform intensive investigations for a living (sniffing out crime), I love Sherlock Holmes. Many years before psychiatrists identified the congruence bias, Sir Arthur Conan Doyle had Holmes explain it to Dr. Watson. In "A Scandal in Bohemia,"

Holmes tells Watson, "It is a capital mistake to theorize before one has data. Insensibly one begins to twist facts to suit theories instead of theories to suit facts."

Tim Lever was especially susceptible to the congruence bias because he did not have enough experience with financial scams for the Ponzi scheme hypothesis to occur to him. In Sherlock Holmes's terms, Tim lacked crucial facts. He therefore fit the few facts that were available into his only theory: that Dennis Golden's investment was legitimate.

Unfortunately, Tim Lever is neither a Sherlock Holmes fan nor a student of the science of decision making. What chance did Tim have to avoid this disaster, then? Was he destined to fall for at least one investment fraud before he could count on his brain to be more help than hindrance? In Tom Brady's terms, did Tim have to throw an interception before he could complete a touchdown pass?

No. Remember that part of what informs Brady's decisions is his study of game films and his practice repetitions. Tim can seed his brain with the interceptions and incompletions thrown by others without throwing one himself. He can study the equivalent of Brady's game films and take the equivalent of Brady's practice snaps by becoming a student of investment scams. By reading blogs like Investor's Watchblog and by reading books like this one, Tim can store in his brain the interceptions of others, the game-film failures that will send forth a negative emotion—an error signal—that will make Tim more cautious about the next investment. Even if Tim decides not to hire a professional investor protection company to investigate his next opportunity, he will remember the scams that he has read about. He will remember that most investment scams look eminently legitimate, and that there is often a positive endorsement from a friend or relative who swears that the investment is real.

Most important, Tim will be conscious of how he evaluates investments. He will be aware of his cognitive biases, sensitive to appeals to his pride, and knowledgeable enough to gather the facts he needs to test the "investment fraud theory." By becoming a vigilant investor, Tim increases his chances of completing enough profitable passes to take him across the retirement goal line.

Due Diligence for the Vigilant

The vigilant investor:

► Understands that all healthy humans are vulnerable to investor fraud

► Discounts the effect of gullibility and resists the temptation to blame the victim

► Is aware of his cognitive biases and compensates for them

► Reads about investment scams to seed his brain with interceptions and incompletions

► Understands that scam artists target accomplished people not just because they have money, but also because it is easier to manipulate their pride

► Remembers that pride leads to *destruction*, not just a fall

► Always considers the "investment fraud" theory along with the "legitimate investment" theory

2

The Posse and the Prey

The Investment Cops and the Scam Artists They Pursue

Intellectuals solve problems; geniuses prevent them.

—ALBERT EINSTEIN

In 1986, Roc "Rocky" G. Hatfield was the 29-year-old chief operating officer of Centuri Mining Corp. (Centuri). Operating from offices in Clearwater, Florida, he advertised Centuri stock for sale via ads in the *Wall Street Journal.* The ads did not warn investors that Centuri had not registered the stock for sale (as required under the federal securities laws). Hatfield told prospective investors that Centuri owned $225 million in gold deposits and mining operations on the Nechi River in Colombia. He sent a report from an "independent geologist" confirming the gold deposits. The report was fake.

The SEC caught on to Hatfield's scam early and filed an emergency enforcement action to shut it down. In August 1989, he consented to an injunction against further violation of the federal securities laws (a "don't-do-it-again order"). The criminal authorities showed no interest. This put an end to Centuri, but it was far from the end of Hatfield's investment scams, which we'll return to soon.

While every scam artist is different, and each brings his own flair and idiosyncrasies to a scheme, we can fit most of them into five broad categories: the Career Criminal, the Golden Boy, the Fibber, the Bungler, and the Thief. In this chapter, we'll look at each, and see how a vigilant investor might recognize one.

But first, let's take a look at the relatively small team of people whose job is tracking down investment fraudsters and bringing them to justice. The members of the team are the SEC; state securities regulators; the FBI; and federal, state, and local prosecutors—you can think of them collectively as the investment cops. From more than 20 years of watching them work, both as a member of that team and off it, I can tell you that they are a dedicated group of true believers, the kind of people you'd be proud to know and have in public service. And, like the Spartans at Thermopylae, they are fighting a holding action against an overwhelming force of investment crooks; no matter how many crooks they strike down, the horde will always keep surging at and around this small band of protectors.

The Investment Cops: Civil and Criminal, Federal and State

Created in the wake of the stock market crash of 1929, the SEC is the primary enforcer of U.S. securities laws.[1] The SEC's Division of Enforcement works on catching securities violators all day, every day. The primary investigators at the SEC are the approximately 600 enforcement attorneys[2] stationed in Washington, D.C., and in the

SEC's 11 regional offices, which stretch from Los Angeles to Boston, from San Francisco to Miami.

The SEC is a civil enforcement agency. It cannot throw violators in prison. Its primary enforcement weapons are don't-do-it-again injunctions, disgorgement,[3] civil penalties, fines, and orders prohibiting violators from working in the securities industry or being an officer or a director of a public company. When appropriate, the SEC asks federal courts to freeze the violator's assets and to appoint a receiver, who works to recover money for eventual distribution to the victims.[4] Even in receivership cases, though, the SEC tells investors that they need to hire a private attorney to represent their individual interests, as the agency cannot seek redress for any individual investor.

While the SEC is supposed to grow as a result of the Dodd-Frank Act of 2010[5] (Dodd-Frank), it will always be frightfully small for the task that confronts it, and it can address only a tiny fraction of the securities violations that occur every day. It tries to make smart choices about what cases to pursue, preferring large, publicity-worthy cases that might deter others from similar conduct. Unless the case threatens the integrity of the markets (for example, insider-trading cases or market manipulation cases), the SEC tends to refer cases involving relatively little money or few investors to its counterparts at the state level. And, as the SEC's miss in the Madoff case illustrates, they are fallible and sometimes miss violations that a deeper investigation might reveal.

Like the SEC, state securities regulators are civil enforcers. Usually divisions of the state secretary of state's office, their primary enforcement tools are cease-and-desist orders, fines, and orders barring violators from acting as a broker or an adviser in their state.

Although lobbyists for the securities industry are always working to limit their authority, state securities regulators are vitally important to investor protection. Between 2005 and 2007,[6] state regulators commenced more than 8,300 enforcement actions;[7] the SEC commenced 1,859. All state regulators belong to the North American Securities Administrators Association (NASAA), along with regulators from Mexico, Puerto Rico, the U.S. Virgin Islands, and every Canadian province. NASAA's web site (www.nasaa.org) is a terrific source of investor protection information and news about emerging investment scams.

Since the economic crisis of 2007, state regulators have been under severe budget pressure. Dodd-Frank will add to their burden. It shifts the responsibility for regulating investment advisers who manage less than $100 million from the SEC to state regulators, which means that the state regulators are now responsible for 4,300 additional investment advisers, when they can barely cover the advisers that they watched before.

Because investment crimes are so lucrative, violators are willing to risk civil sanctions for the chance at the profits from their scams. Prison is the only effective deterrent. The FBI and state and local law enforcement can arrest investment scamsters, and prosecutors can bring them to trial. However, securing convictions is harder than it appears on *Law & Order*. Prosecutors must prove criminal intent beyond a reasonable doubt.[8] Although there is never a shortage of aggrieved investors who are willing to testify, none of them can take the jury inside the accused's head. Defendants often claim that they were simply mistaken about what the investment could do. "I'm as outraged as the investors at how we were all misled," is a common refrain. To get a conviction, the prosecutor has to prove that the defendant acted knowingly. And, given that investment fraud has gone global, prosecutors often have to find witnesses and documents overseas, an expensive proposition for a county prosecutor's office.

Add to that the strictures of the rules of evidence, and getting a conviction in an investment fraud case is difficult.

Like the civil enforcers, criminal authorities have more work than they can handle. Even agents and prosecutors who are specifically assigned to white-collar crime units have cases involving embezzlement, counterfeiting, bribery, accounting fraud, computer hacking, and other crimes competing with investment fraud cases for their attention. It is little wonder, then, that prosecutors sometimes conclude that civil sanctions will have to be enough.

Despite the investment cops' best efforts, there are gaping holes in the securities enforcement structure through which violators often slip, moving from state to state—and often overseas—to escape capture and prosecution. Even quadrupling the size of the enforcement team probably would not deter the characters we'll describe in this chapter.

A vigilant investor thinks of the investment cops as homicide detectives. It's after midnight. They get a call about a crime committed in an upper-middle-class suburb. They park on the curb, duck under the crime scene tape, flash their credentials, and approach the sheet-covered lump on the living room floor. Under the sheet, they find a pile of nest eggs that have been scrambled beyond all recognition. They follow the leads and, in almost all cases, bring someone to justice. The perpetrator might go to prison, or she might get off with a civil penalty. But, like all the king's horses and all the king's men, the investment cops cannot put the nest eggs together again. They chalk the case up as a win because they solved it, called the bad guys to account for their crimes, and stopped them from killing again . . . for a little while. Justice does its job, but it cannot undo a crime. That is why every vigilant investor makes prevention his first priority.

The Career Criminal

By August 1993, Roc Hatfield had put Centuri Mining Corp. behind him and become the chief executive officer of a company called Marada Capital, Inc. (Marada). Marada was a brokerage operation with salespeople in seven cities, but Hatfield never registered it as a broker-dealer (again, something that the law requires). Given his prior experience with the SEC, the chances are good that it did not simply slip his mind.

Marada sold (unregistered) stock in subsidiaries Marada Air, Inc., and Marada Casino Resort Hotels, Inc. Hatfield hired telemarketers, whom he called "brokers," gave them sales scripts and glossy brochures, and motivated them to use high-pressure sales tactics by paying a 40 percent commission on each sale. Being more than sufficiently motivated, Marada "brokers" told investors that the company had exclusive agreements with Caribbean island nations to operate and develop an airline, casinos, and hotels in those countries—none of which was true. Hatfield sold $2 million in Marada stock at $1 per share to 200 investors, failing to mention his prior trouble with the SEC.

Again moving quickly, the SEC shut down Hatfield's latest operation through an emergency enforcement action in September 1994, securing another don't-do-it-again order and an order requiring Hatfield to disgorge (surrender) $1,941,000. The SEC also filed a proceeding against Hatfield to officially kick him out of the securities industry (which he had never properly entered).

The SEC was not the only Investment Cop that was fed up with Hatfield. Based on the illegal activity run out of Marada's boiler room (a room equipped with telephones, computer terminals, and salespeople using high-pressure sales tactics), California prosecutors secured a criminal conviction against him for fraud and illegal securities trading, resulting in a sentence of two years in prison. He served his time in the state prison system and was released in 1998.

A few years later, in 2002, no one at the SEC was surprised to learn that Hatfield had been selling "notes" in a company called Global Diamond Fund (GDF) since September 2001, telling investors that their investments were secured by South African diamond operations. Rather than seek yet another don't-do-it-again order, the SEC pursued a contempt of court order for violation of the Marada order. Whether because of a lack of resources, the prospect of having to gather evidence from South Africa, or an assessment that they could not prove criminal intent, the criminal authorities did not pursue Hatfield for GDF. He spent less than two weeks in prison for contempt of the second don't-do-it-again order.[9]

You might think that characters like Hatfield are rare, but they are everywhere. You may believe that they are easy to spot if you aren't prone to being sucked in by every get-rich-quick scheme, but that's what the Career Criminal is counting on.

Professional scam artists put in long hours of planning and preparation before they talk to their first mark. If you want to get an idea of how much goes into creating a successful scam, watch *The Sting* (winner of the Oscar for Best Picture in 1973) or *The Spanish Prisoner*, written by David Mamet. There are offices to rent, equipment to buy, employees to hire, web sites to design, phone lines to staff, documents to create, and enough boring paperwork to put a meth addict to sleep.

The Career Criminal is not a fast-talking, fly-by-the-seat-of-the-pants type. He is exceptionally intelligent, is detail-oriented, has a near-photographic memory, is exceptionally good at picking up on verbal and nonverbal clues to what you are thinking and feeling, and can adapt his pitch on a dime in response to your reactions. In the

1986 movie *The Color of Money*, Paul Newman's character describes a master hustler as "a student of human moves." There is not a more apt description of the skill that career con artists bring to their work.

The Career Criminal is a chameleon, not unlike a CIA agent, trained to "blend in." When not convincing someone to give up state secrets, a CIA agent's number one assignment is, "Live your cover." The career scam artist does the same, working as an insurance agent, a real estate agent, an accountant, a stockbroker, or whatever. He will live the lie so convincingly that it becomes real for him . . . and for you.

As Hatfield's story shows, you are safe from Career Criminals only when they are in prison, and even then you are at risk from the day of their release.

Reading Roc Hatfield's story may leave you feeling frustrated at the SEC's inability to stop a scam artist from spinning fraudulent scheme after fraudulent scheme. But trust me, no one is more frustrated by individuals like Hatfield than the SEC. Unfortunately, as a civil enforcement agency, it does not have the legal authority to throw violators in prison. Its enforcement options are limited to injunctions, monetary judgments, and orders kicking violators out of the securities industry. Those did not stop Hatfield, and they will not stop any Career Criminal.

Avoiding a Career Criminal begins with an understanding that you cannot recognize one by her appearance. What Depression-era bank teller Homer Edgeworth said about George "Machine Gun" Kelly applies equally to financial scamsters: "He was the kind of guy that, if you looked at him, you never would have thought he was a bank robber." Luckily, looking into an investment promoter's past can tell you what physical appearance cannot. A couple of web sites can help.

A search function available on the SEC's web address, www.sec .gov, will bring up prior enforcement actions. By looking at it, Hatfield's victims in the Marada and GDF frauds could have learned about the earlier don't-do-it-again order against him in the Centuri Mining case. However, searching the SEC's web site would *not* have revealed Hatfield's criminal conviction in California. Had that been Hatfield's only previous violation, only a courthouse records search in California would have uncovered it.

Although investors cannot access all state criminal convictions online, they can search for federal convictions at www.pacer.gov, an electronic public access service that allows users to obtain case and docket information from federal, district, and bankruptcy courts. There is a small fee, but the search results are pulled straight from the docket of every federal case. A search of courthouse records—whether federal records through PACER (Public Access to Court Electronic Records) or a physical search of each courthouse in counties in which the subject has lived or done business—can also reveal prior lawsuits against the subject. A Career Criminal often leaves a trail of civil judgments.

Unless you are qualified to do so by training and experience, it's wise never to base investment decisions on your assessment of whether the investment promoter is telling the truth. Many Career Criminals are clinical sociopaths.[10] They do not display the indicators of stress that are present in the vast majority of people when they lie. Only an experienced investigator can flush them out.

But do pay attention to that bad feeling you get when you consider the investment. It isn't indigestion. It's your brain recognizing reasons why you should avoid it. You may not yet be able to articulate that feeling, but you should listen to it.

The Golden Boy

Kirk S. Wright earned a master's degree in public policy from the Kennedy School of Government at Harvard University in 1995. Thirteen years later, on May 24, 2008, he hung himself in his cell at the Union City jail near Atlanta after being convicted of defrauding hundreds of people out of more than $185 million through his seven hedge funds. The most visible of Wright's victims were current and former players in the National Football League (NFL), but they accounted for only about $20 million of the money that Wright took. His other victims included doctors, retirees, business executives . . . and his mother.

Just one year out of college, Wright left a job that he had landed at a Washington, D.C., consulting firm to start a hedge fund firm that he called International Management Associates (IMA). Though he started out in his basement, he eventually opened offices in New York, Los Angeles, Las Vegas, and Atlanta, where he moved in 2000.

Wright's credentials and his gift of connecting with people brought him clients early on. By showing impressive returns, he gained introductions to new prospects. In the late 1990s, Wright drew close to a pair of Atlanta-based anesthesiologists who became clients and, ultimately, partners in IMA. They introduced him to other doctors and set up seminars nationwide at which Wright impressed the audience with charts and graphs illustrating his success.

Wright took pains to impress everyone he met. He rented luxury suites at Atlanta Hawks and Atlanta Falcons games and entertained prospective clients there. He bought luxury automobiles, including a Jaguar and an Aston Martin. He bought and expanded a house at the end of a cul-de-sac in suburban Atlanta.

By 2004, Wright had succeeded in getting himself on the list of approved financial advisers kept by the NFL Players Association (NFLPA), the union for NFL players.[11] Not long afterward, a satisfied IMA investor told NFL veteran Steve Atwater about IMA. Seeing the impressive returns that IMA reported and that Wright was on the NFLPA's list of approved advisers, Atwater introduced several of his former NFL teammates to IMA.

Wright's primary investment approach was short selling (borrowing shares and selling them in anticipation of a drop in the stock price, after which the short seller buys the stock back at the lower price). His trades, however, were unsuccessful, and all of his funds lost staggering sums.

Although Wright restricted access to the brokerage account statements that showed his unsuccessful trading, the CPA for his funds eventually gained access to the brokerage statements and found discrepancies between the trades on those statements and the returns that Wright was reporting. Not long afterward, the Atlanta offices of the SEC and the FBI began investigating. On May 17, 2007, the FBI found Wright lounging by the swimming pool at the Ritz-Carlton on South Beach in Miami and arrested him. He was ultimately convicted by a federal jury on 47 counts of mail fraud, securities fraud, and money laundering. Facing a prison sentence of up to 710 years, he committed suicide. He was 37 years old.

The Golden Boy[12] begins young. You'll be impressed by his energy and his charisma. In addition to paying for his own luxurious lifestyle, the Golden Boy will often give lavishly to charity. His upscale lifestyle will catch your attention, and you'll be tempted to chalk it up to his investing prowess. Don't. If your investment adviser spends money like a trust fund baby on a weekend shopping bender, he is spending your money, not his own.

Just as DEA agents use a profile to identify drug mules flying in from foreign countries, the vigilant investor compares a prospective investment adviser to the profile of the Golden Boy. Does he give to charity, ensuring that he gets credit for it? Does he spend money in a way that draws attention? Does he have an impressive pedigree to live up to? Is he vain? Does he wear tailored suits? Does he have the best of everything? If the answer is yes, stay away.

The Golden Boy will resist requests for transparency, but the vigilant investor will insist on it. If you ask for backup information on the trades that supposedly generated the profits or ask to speak to the fund's auditor, the Golden Boy will stall, dissemble, or storm, feigning anger at your lack of trust. If he cannot charm or intimidate you out of insisting on that transparency, he might say, "That's just not the way it's done." The vigilant investor responds, "If you want my money, that *is* the way it's done." In the wake of the Madoff scandal, the investment promoter must either provide more transparency or live with the consequences of the presumption that he is another Madoff in the making. If you get any of the other reactions covered here, walk away. Better yet, take your money and run.

If, like Kirk Wright's hedge funds, the investment you are considering supposedly makes money from trading stocks, bonds, or other securities, ask to see the most recent month's brokerage statement. Because you remember what you learned about the congruence bias from Chapter 1, you will consider the possibility that the statement is phony; technology has made it relatively easy to produce genuine-looking fakes. Here is how we identify a phony statement.

Like a bank statement, every brokerage statement has a beginning date and an ending date. It's the ending date you are interested in. Let's assume that the ending date for the statement in front of you is June 30, 2010, and that the statement shows that the closing price of Apple, Inc., on that day was $275. Many free online sources can give you the actual closing price of the stock.[13] Does the actual closing price match what the statement shows? If so, move on to the next stock in the fund; the Golden Boy might not lie about every stock in the fund, only those that are trending downward. If the prices do not match—if the actual closing price of Apple on that date was $251.53—you've found a Golden Boy. Call the closest SEC regional office,[14] call Investor's Watchdog, and pat yourself on the back for saving not only your nest egg but probably hundreds of others.

Ask your financial adviser when the fund was last audited and who performed the audit. Call the auditor. The auditor probably will not give you much information, but he should at least be willing to confirm the audit. You might find out that the auditor has never heard of the fund.

If the auditing firm confirms the audit, investigate the auditing firm. A fund with several hundred million dollars will require an accounting firm with a substantial staff. If the auditor is a one- or two-man operation, it simply cannot possibly perform the work required for a meaningful audit. Remember that Bernard Madoff's auditor, Friehling & Horowitz, was a very small operation in New City, New York, an hour up the Hudson River from Manhattan.

Pay attention to the fund's marketing materials as well. Do they describe the investment manager's methodology? Does that methodology make economic sense, or is it indecipherable industry jargon? Kirk Wright once described the methodology for the IMA Platinum Fund as follows: "The Platinum Fund seeks to capitalize volumetrically on a few select opportunities characterized by moderate to high valuations, compelling business fundamentals, and strong management teams." Golden Boys often use jargon-laced language. No matter what your level of education or experience, you should be able to understand how the manager makes money with your money. If you do not, it may be because a Golden Boy is being deliberately obtuse, hiding his scam behind an explanation full of technical-sounding industry terms.

The Fibber

There is another breed of scam artist that is just as dangerous as the Career Criminal and the Golden Boy, but harder to recognize. Many of the fraudulent hedge funds that came to light in the wake of the economic collapse were created not by professional scam artists or ego-driven achievers, but by registered investment advisers who started out with good intentions. A single moment of poor judgment—an isolated mistake, if you ask them—led them across the line that divides legitimate businesspeople from scam operators.

The investment advisory business is competitive. Advisers battle one another like Ali and Frazier, always worried that the competition will steal the clients whose assets generate the fees that pay the adviser's mortgage.

Consider the case of Charles Lee Harris and his company, Tradewinds International, LLC (Tradewinds). Harris lived in the tony lakefront suburb of Winnetka, Illinois. Beginning in 1995, he operated Tradewinds and its successor companies as a commodity pool, investing in commodity futures and options. He raised $23 million from 30 investors, sending them monthly statements showing the results of his trading. From 1996 to the summer of 2004, Harris's investors were pleased with the returns that he reported.

Things changed on July 18, 2004. On that date, one of Harris's investors received a digitally recorded video in the mail. He put the

DVD into his computer and saw Harris's face. Speaking into the camera, apparently from one of his boats, Harris said, "Last year we didn't have a good year and I . . . bottom line is that last year, when we thought we were up 12 percent, I, ah, I knew we weren't up 12 percent, and actually we ended up being down 8 percent. . . . I am so sick and f#$%ing tired of lying."

Tracing Harris's cell phone signal, the FBI found him on his boat in the Turks and Caicos Islands. He voluntarily returned to the United States and pleaded guilty to one count of wire fraud, no doubt expecting a light sentence in exchange for saving the government the expense of a trial. Instead, U.S. District Judge Matthew F. Kennelly sentenced Harris to 168 months in prison. He gets out in November 2016, or a few months sooner if he behaves himself. As inmate number 21684-424 at the Federal Correctional Institution in Petersburg, Virginia, Harris no doubt regrets that one moment in which he thought it better to lie than to admit a loss.

A single poor choice leads scores—possibly hundreds—of otherwise honest investment managers to become scam artists every year. Like Harris, in the wake of what they think of as an isolated white lie, they take more risk with their clients' investments, hoping to make up for the losses that they lied about. But taking longer risks always comes with an increased exposure to larger losses. Inevitably they lose everything in their effort to hide a relatively modest loss.

The Fibber does not want to disappoint you because her income depends upon your leaving your money under her control. The Fibber gets a percentage of it every year. You may be able to help remove the temptation that leads the Fibber to tell that first lie by saying up front that losses that are consistent with your risk tolerance are understandable. But you cannot know whether another investor is tempting the adviser to cross that ethical line.

An investment adviser with few clients has a more powerful motivation to lie if the investments he makes take a precipitous drop. Every client who leaves takes away a significant part of the adviser's income. You therefore want to find out how many clients your prospective adviser has. Form ADV (the ADV), which the adviser must file annually with the SEC or with state regulators, gives that and other important information. While the law requires every adviser to give you a copy of his ADV, the vigilant investor gets it not only from his adviser, but also from regulators at www.adviserinfo.sec.gov. Compare the number of clients listed on the ADV that you get from regulators with the number that the adviser gives you. If the adviser gives you a significantly higher number than he reported to the SEC, you have uncovered a tendency to fib. Stay away. If the numbers match, ask the adviser whether he has a client whose account represents more than 5 percent of his assets under management. If so, he may be tempted to keep that investor happy at all costs.

Spotting the Fibber before you give her your money is hard. The best you can do is look for the motivation to lie. The vigilant investor does that by comparing the adviser's lifestyle with her approximate income to determine how much margin that lifestyle allows for a drop in income. That comparison begins with finding out how the adviser gets paid.

Most investment advisers earn a percentage of their assets under management (AUM), the sum of all of their clients' assets. Hedge fund managers typically earn a percentage of profits as well. The ADV and/or the private placement memorandum will spell out how the adviser or manager gets paid. The adviser's management fee generally ranges between 1 and 2 percent per year. You can learn an adviser's AUM by looking at his ADV. By multiplying the adviser's annual fee by his assets under management, you can approximate his annual revenue. Subtract from that the approximate expenses of his operation—taxes, rent, insurance, and payroll—and you will know approximately how much your adviser takes home.[15] Unless his spouse has a high-paying job (something that you can learn while exchanging the pleasantries that precede a discussion of business), an adviser with a relatively modest income and few clients cannot afford an exodus of clients if his lifestyle includes private school for the kids, country club membership, and a late-model luxury car. If the investments that the adviser chooses take a hard fall, he will be powerfully tempted to fib. After the first lie, the lie—not sound investment principles—drives every investment decision.

This same analysis can unmask any variety of scamster. An adviser with an approximate income of $200,000 cannot afford to be the top donor to the United Way, drive luxury cars, maintain a beach house, and pilot a yacht while sending his children to elite schools. Where is the money coming from? You know where.

The Bungler

Thomas Repke did not graduate from college. He left one credit hour short of graduation. He would tell you that his failure to obtain a degree was completely irrelevant to his qualifications to handle the four investment funds he managed through the Salt Lake City offices of Coadum Advisers, Inc.

James Jeffery, a Canadian citizen with experience in the insurance business, was Repke's partner in Coadum. Jeffery had had no experience managing other people's money when he and Repke decided to launch the Coadum funds in 2006.

Repke and Jeffery believed that they could generate large returns.

Their research had led them to several investments called "high-yield investments" that promised risk-free returns on short-term investments. They did the math and calculated how much they could return to investors if those opportunities paid off as promised and how much they could make from the management fees and profit participation. They cobbled together a private placement memorandum, hired some salespeople, and set about raising money from investors for the Coadum 1 Fund. Having raised more than $1 million in that fund, they promptly gave it to an attorney in Houston who was representing one of the high-yield investments. The person behind the investment, based in Europe, stole the money.

Undaunted, Repke and Jeffery continued raising money, creating Coadum Fund II, Coadum Fund III, and Mansell Capital Partners. They ultimately raised $38 million. They sent $19 million of it to Europe (Malta and Switzerland), where yet another scam artist stole it. Based on promises from the European scamsters, Repke and Jeffery sent their investors false account statements showing that their investments were earning the promised return. The money never arrived and never will, and close to 200 people lost their life savings because of the actions of two inexperienced low-level businessmen. In December 2010, Repke and Jeffery were indicted on 22 counts of mail fraud, wire fraud, and conspiracy.

David A. Dunning, Ph.D. (professor of psychology at Cornell), and Justin Kruger, Ph.D. (assistant professor of psychology at the University of Illinois), suggest an explanation for how two sentient adults could fall for two separate investment scams within the span of 12 months, yet still believe that they were competent to manage other people's money. Covering the story for the *New York Times*, reporter Erica Goode wrote, "People who do things badly, Dr. Dunning has found . . . are usually supremely confident of their abilities—more confident, in fact, than people who do things well." The central explanation for this finding is that "the skills required for competence often are the same skills necessary to recognize competence." On the other side of the equation, psychologists long ago identified what they call the "false consensus effect," in which highly competent people tend to believe that everyone else is as competent as they are, thereby *underrating* their own competence.

Investors who are determined to avoid the Bungler must investigate his background. Does this person really have the educational credentials that she claims? Beware of anyone who claims a Ph.D. from the School of Life or its sister institution, the School of Hard Knocks, even if you earned your own degree there. Has this person ever done this kind of thing before? If so, how did it go? Record the answers, but don't believe them, yet.

Bunglers know that credentials—education, experience, and designations such as CFP[16] or CFA[17]—are important to investors. They will often describe their educational background in ways that lead an inattentive reader to make inaccurate assumptions. An adviser who boasts that she "*attended* the University of Virginia" may have attended for two semesters before being suspended for poor academic performance. If an adviser's marketing materials say, "After leaving Georgetown University, Bill Bungler took a job on Wall Street," most readers will assume that Bungler had earned a degree from Georgetown and taken a job with an investment-banking firm.

There is no room for assumptions in vigilant investing. Unless the adviser tells you the specific degree he obtained, ask him what degree he earned. Ask also for his title and employer in that job he took "on Wall Street." More than one hot dog vendor can accurately claim to have worked on Wall Street. If you catch someone trying to lead you to false assumptions, that is reason enough to stay away from any investment that he is offering.[18]

Although the vigilant investor asks questions and writes down the answers that an adviser provides, she does not rely on them. Instead, the vigilant investor seeks independent confirmation. At Investor's Watchdog, we get education information from the National Student Clearinghouse (NSC). If you give the NSC an accurate birth date, student name, school name, and $6.50, it will either confirm what your adviser told you about his education or expose the Fibber.

If your adviser supposedly makes money by trading securities, you can unmask a Bungler by doing a simple calculation. You will need brokerage account statements for the past year to do the calculation independently.[19] You are going to calculate the *turnover rate* for the fund. The turnover rate measures how often the manager executes trades in the account. Incompetent managers trade too often (they are convinced that they can time the market) and damage the performance of the fund by creating massive commission charges.[20]

The most frequently traded legitimate hedge funds have a turnover rate of around 1. If your manager has a higher turnover rate, she is probably trading the account too often, pushing the break-even point farther out by incurring large commission charges. Of course, because she lacks the ability to appreciate her own incompetence, she may never realize how much her frequent trading is costing the fund.

To find the turnover rate, find the average equity of the account by adding up the total value of the account—usually listed as "ending equity" on the front page of the monthly brokerage statement—for the past 12 months and dividing by 12. Now add up the value of the "buy" transactions during those 12 months; ignore the "sell" transactions. Divide the total purchases by the average equity and you have the turnover rate. A turnover rate above 1 should make you suspicious. A turnover rate of 3 should send you looking for another investment manager immediately. I have seen turnover rates higher than 100.

If you cannot get access to several months of statements, you might be able to spot a Bungler from a single brokerage statement. Successful traders tend to hold their winners and sell their losers. Incompetent traders do it the other way around. If the brokerage statement shows large unrealized losses, you might be dealing with a Bungler who is unwilling to sell his losing positions because, he tells himself, "If I don't sell them, they aren't really losses."

Finally, you might be able to spot a Bungler by paying attention to whether the return on the investment depends upon the performance of someone you have not met. Too often, Bunglers promise attractive returns based on assurances from professional scam artists. If the offering document for the investment describes a profit-generating process over which your investment adviser has no control, you may have found a Bungler who has been sucked into a scam, just the way Repke and Jeffery were—twice.

Investors in funds of funds (hedge funds that invest in other hedge funds) can easily lose money to a Bungler. Unless those investors investigate every hedge fund in which their fund invests, they cannot rest assured that an inept manager has not given their money to a cleverly disguised scam. Professor Stephen Greenspan (the gullibility expert that we discussed in Chapter 1) entrusted his money to a fund-of-funds manager who sent it to Bernard Madoff. Had Professor Greenspan known that, and followed the advice in this book, he would have found more red flags flying over Madoff's office than he would have been comfortable with.

The Thief

As frauds go, Homer Forster's was plain vanilla—a straight theft. Homer had invested his clients' nest eggs in variable annuities. In December 1993, he forged redemption requests to the annuity companies, directing them to liquidate the investments and send the proceeds to his business, the Center for Financial Planning. With $1.6 million of his clients' money in hand, Homer and his girlfriend fled the United States with phony passports that they had acquired in the weeks leading up to the theft. I got the case while I was an enforcement branch chief at the SEC.

We sent Homer's name and physical description to the U.S. Customs Service quickly, but Homer and his girlfriend slipped across the border with the phony passports. They fled to Luxembourg, where they collected the money that they had stolen and wired ahead. They ultimately settled in Estepona, Spain, on the Mediterranean coast.

Homer was on the lam for 10 years but was finally arrested by Interpol agents in Dubai. He pleaded guilty to mail and wire fraud and was sentenced to serve 51 months in prison. He was released in May 2009.

Whether responding to a middle-aged psychosis or an inexorable sociopathic desire for immediate self-gratification, the Thief wants your money without the hassles and hard work required of the Career Criminal. Like a purse snatcher, he is on the lowest level of the criminal hierarchy. He's not a craftsman—just a brute. Unlike the purse snatcher, though, the white-collar Thief must do at least enough work to put herself in a position to steal from you.

Because she is often registered as a broker or an investment adviser, the quest to unmask a Thief requires going beyond checking to make sure that she is properly licensed, but it should begin there.

If the adviser is offering investment advice or selling investments, she must be registered to do so in your state. You can learn whether an adviser has the proper license by contacting your state's securities commissioner and asking for a copy of the subject's Central Registration Depository (CRD) report. That report will list the subject's licenses and the states in which she may sell investments. If the securities commissioner reports that the office has no record of the person who is trying to sell you an investment, ask to speak to enforcement personnel and give them the details.

The vigilant investor never relies on the BrokerCheck database maintained by the Financial Industry Regulatory Authority (FINRA). That database does not include the thousands of customer complaints and arbitration awards entered against stockbrokers who negotiated to have those actions expunged from their records. FINRA's Broker-Check is beyond useless; it is dangerous. Investor's Watchdog investigated one stockbroker who appeared to have a completely clean record on BrokerCheck, but who had 10 separate customer complaints in the IW database. How many customers gave their nest egg to that broker, believing that she had never harmed a single investor?

Unfortunately, it is not at all unusual for the Thief to earn the proper licenses before pulling his first job. Pay attention, therefore, to how an adviser tells you to pay for an investment. No legitimate financial adviser will ask you to write a check to him personally.[21] In fact, only an amateur Thief would ask you to do something that is so obviously out of the ordinary. The experienced Thief will ask you to write your check to a corporation that sounds investment-related, for instance, First Securities Corp. of California, Inc., or Bailey Trust Group, LLC. Before you hand over your money, you must know whether there is, in fact, such a business and, if so, whether the adviser controls it. Writing a check to a business that the adviser controls is the same as writing a check to the adviser personally.

Start with your state secretary of state's office. All such offices have web sites that allow you to research businesses that are registered to operate in the state. Plug in the name of the business your adviser identified. Is the address of the business the same as that of your adviser's home or business? If so, you have caught a potential Thief and saved your nest egg.[22]

The secretary of state's web site can help you catch a Thief one other way. Search for the name of the adviser. Most states will tell you whether she is listed as an officer or a director of any other businesses.[23] Make a note of any that you find and ask the adviser what they do. If they are defunct businesses, there may be disappointed former partners or investors who are pressing the adviser for repayment of a loan or an investment. Ask the adviser whether she had any partners or investors in the prior business and why the business closed. If the adviser has active businesses, the Thief might be tempted to "borrow" your money to see those businesses through a "temporary" cash crunch. Moreover, finding out about outside businesses is important because if your adviser cannot devote her full attention to the investment she is asking you to buy, you do not want to invest in it.

You can also protect yourself from the Thief by looking at your bank statements, if you have an account that allows you to see copies of your canceled checks. Look at the check you wrote for the investment. Is it still made out as you wrote it, or has it been altered to be made payable to someone else? Check the back. Did your investment adviser or someone else endorse the check? If so, you have caught a Thief. The faster you report the crime, the more likely it is that you will recover your money.

Because identifying a Thief in advance is so challenging, you should pay attention to whether the Thief works for a business that will compensate you if the Thief takes your money to the Caribbean. Ask yourself, "If this person pulls a Steve Miller Band ("Take the Money and Run"), what financially stable company would a court order to return my money?" If no one comes to mind, you are at heightened risk from a Thief.

Due Diligence for the Vigilant

The vigilant investor:

▶ Does not count on the investment cops to keep her safe

▶ Says no to every high-pressure sales pitch and never invests based solely on an Internet or a telephone solicitation

▶ Investigates the people behind the proposed investment, using regulatory web sites and documents, and courthouse records searches

▶ Avoids advisers who spend as if money will be worthless tomorrow

▶ Insists on seeing evidence of profitable trading (such as brokerage statements) and avoids anyone who is unwilling to be transparent

▶ Checks for phony account or brokerage statements and avoids people who try to suggest credentials that they do not have

▶ Assesses whether the adviser has clients who account for a big percentage of his income and whether the adviser's lifestyle will motivate him to fib if he loses clients

▶ Assesses an adviser's competence by confirming education through the NSC, employment history by calling former employers, and investment history through courthouse records searches

▶ Checks for proper licensing by getting a CRD from state regulators, pays attention to how she pays for investments, and does business with companies that can pay back what a thief might take

3

Rich Man, Poor Man

An Investment Scam for Every Economic Bracket

A rich man is nothing but a poor man with money.

—W. C. Fields

Harold Glantz was a New York "businessman"—the president of a chain of bagel stores whose stock offering was suspended by the SEC—with ties to the Gambino and Genovese crime families. A 1976 letter from the New York City commissioner of investigation, Nicholas Scoppetta, to the New York Economic Development Administration concluded that "Glantz has been associated with high-level organized crime figures and has apparently served as agent for them in encroachment on legitimate business interests."

In 1992, Glantz convinced Stuart Ford and Gamil Naguib, financial advisers to the Salvation Army in the United Kingdom, that he had access to a "risk-free trading platform" that could generate a profit of $650,000 in only a few weeks. Passing along information that they had learned from Glantz, the two told Salvation Army fund-raiser Colonel Grenville Burn and his superiors about a highly exclusive market for instruments called "standby letters of credit." Ford and Naguib convinced Burn that the market was so exclusive that only the top 10 banks in the world ("prime banks"), governments, and very wealthy individuals had access to it. The advisers told Burn that Glantz's trader could buy a standby letter of credit for $4,350,000 and immediately sell it for its face value of $5 million. However, Glantz had other plans for the Salvation Army's money.

Glantz was operating a *prime bank scam*—a scam so virulent that, despite the unrelenting work of civil and criminal enforcement authorities the world over, it continues to thrive, preying mostly on charities, endowments, pension funds, hedge funds, and wealthy individuals.[1] In this chapter, we will look at the prime bank scam, as well as hedge fund frauds, scam mall frauds, the recovery scam, and the giveaway scam. From institutional investors to the financially desperate, we will identify the kind of investors who are most often targeted by each type of scam and see how the vigilant investor identifies these scams and avoids them.

Prime Bank Scams

The Salvation Army had plans for the $4,350,000 that Glantz proposed to invest for it. The organization needed it to build residential facilities in five major British cities to care for the down-and-out, those who were trying to break their addiction to drugs or alcohol, and elderly citizens who were too sick and impoverished to live on their own. Having the extra $650,000 that Glantz promised would allow them to expand one or more of those residential facilities. Colonel Burn took the idea to his superiors, and they approved the deal.

After passing through three Luxembourg banks, the Salvation Army's money stopped in the Netherlands in the account of a company run by Guido Haak, an associate of Glantz's. Haak contacted an English barrister who ran a small family law practice in Cornwall and had him open several British bank accounts, into which the money was transferred.[2] From there, investigators tracked the money to the United States, into accounts controlled by Glantz, who used $400,000 to buy a Santa Monica, California, apartment for his daughter and the rest as a down payment on a $5 million, eight-bedroom, four-bath house on the Pacific Coast Highway in Malibu.

When the promised returns never appeared, the Salvation Army contacted the U.K.'s Serious Fraud Office (SFO). The SFO pieced together the story and shared its findings with the U.S. Justice Department, which indicted Glantz for wire fraud, conspiracy, and money laundering. Glantz ultimately pleaded guilty to charges stemming from his prime bank fraud. He spent 40 months in federal custody and served three years on supervised release. The court ordered him to sell his Manhattan co-op and ordered other assets (including the Santa Monica apartment and the Malibu house) forfeited to the government in partial satisfaction of an order that he pay restitution of more than $21 million. As of this writing, he is 78 years old and lives with his wife in New Jersey. While there had been versions of the prime bank scam as far back as the 1950s, Glantz's Salvation Army score marked the modern resurgence of the scam.

Like stand-up comedians, prime bank scamsters change their material to appeal to those who may have seen the act before. The changes make the latest scam appear different from the last one exposed in the media. These tweaks help the scam artist allay the fears of investors who have heard of prime bank scams. "Yes," the scam artist will say, "I've read about those scams, too. But they involved supposed 'bank debentures.' How ridiculous! We are trading irrevocable pay orders backed by the International Monetary Fund. You can't get safer than that."

To keep the scam fresh and less detectable, scam artists change the name of the financial instruments that are supposedly being traded to generate the profits. "Standby letters of credit" and "prime bank notes" become "medium-term notes," "irrevocable letters of credit," "bank guarantees," "bank debentures," or "irrevocable pay orders." They change the general description of the program from a "prime bank note program" to a "blocked funds investment program," a "Federal Reserve–approved debenture program," or a "roll programme" (notice the very cosmopolitan British spelling). Seeking to add legitimacy, prime bank scamsters have begun claiming involvement by, or even guarantees from, the World Bank, the International Chamber of Commerce, or the International Monetary Fund.

While the particulars of the description change, the basics of the prime bank scam remain the same. The central pillar on which the entire scam rests is a secret market for little-known financial instruments. Of course, neither the market nor the instruments actually exist.

Confidentiality is a hallmark of these scams. The pitchman says that the identity of the trader and the terms of the program are strictly confidential. Often the investor signs a document providing for a $1 million penalty if he divulges any information about the program. When the expected return never arrives, the fear of the penalty deters the investor from calling regulators just long enough to allow the scamster to launder the money more thoroughly. The fear of that penalty even leads some investors to refuse to talk to the SEC.

The paperwork associated with a prime bank scam often appears to be concerned with determining whether the *investor* is legitimate.

The scamster will insist on proof that the investor's funds are "of good, clean, clear, and noncriminal origin." Notice how this shifts the investor's focus to proving her own legitimacy and away from assessing the legitimacy of the investment.

One of the most pernicious recent additions to the scam involves assuring investors that their funds will "never be put at risk," but will instead be held in an escrow account, against which the trader will borrow in order to make the necessary trades. The guarantee that their money will not leave the escrow account, even if the trader defaults on the supposed loan, is often the tipping point for prime bank victims. What could go wrong if the money is locked up in escrow and can't be touched? Of course, the supposed escrow agent is a cohort of the prime bank scamster and will release the money to the scamster as soon as it hits the account.

This latest accretion to the prime bank scam leads us to one way in which a vigilant investor can recognize the scam for what it is. Think about the promise that your money will remain in an escrow account and that the trader will borrow against it for the cash necessary to make the supposedly profitable trades. If the investors' funds are locked up in an escrow account and cannot be moved under any circumstances, what lender would agree to accept those funds as collateral for the loan that will fund the trading? You do not have to be a bank to understand that collateral that cannot be seized in the event of default is worthless. A lender who would make that loan lives not in the financial capitals of Europe, but in the land of leprechauns and unicorns.

While the prime bank scamster will stress the complexity of the transaction, even a Nobel Prize–winning economist would not be able to understand how the investment could generate a profit; jargon-laced gibberish is incomprehensible to even the brightest mind. The prime bank scamster counts on your prideful willingness either to pretend that you understand his explanation or to believe that some of the highly confidential details of the program, which the scamster cannot disclose, would make it clear. The vigilant investor knows that she is bright enough to understand any legitimate investment and refuses to invest in anything that she does not understand.

Prime bank scams are only one type of what we call the "long con"—a scam that aims to relieve one or a limited number of victims of large sums.[3] Because the long con shoots for a big score, its practitioners target very wealthy individuals, pension funds, endowments, charities, and even Wall Street investment banks.

More and more frequently, practitioners of the long con, including prime bank scamsters, are targeting hedge funds[4] because they give the scamster one-stop convenience. Hedge funds gather investments from investors as big as multibillion-dollar public pension funds and as small as comfortably retired senior citizens, all of which agree to give the hedge fund manager absolute control of all investment decisions.

Hedge Fund Frauds

Over the past 30 years, 40 people have jumped to their deaths from the Bear Mountain Bridge, 40 miles north of Manhattan, into the Hudson River, 150 feet below. So, on the morning of June 9, 2008, when they found a burgundy GMC Envoy parked on the shoulder of the bridge with the keys in the ignition and "suicide is painless" scrawled in the dust and pollen on the hood, police began looking for a body in the river. When they learned that the SUV belonged to Samuel Israel III (Israel), who was supposed to report to prison in

Massachusetts that day, they also began investigating the possibility that Israel had faked his suicide and was on the run from the law.

Israel had roots in New Orleans, where his family had founded a successful commodities trading firm back when some of the employees were Civil War veterans. Prosperity had led the family to New York, where Israel grew up in a house that backed up to the third hole of the Westchester Country Club's south course. After high school, he went back to New Orleans to attend Tulane University and then returned to New York, where he took a job as an entry-level securities trader. In 1996, when he decided to open his own hedge fund, Israel reached back to his New Orleans roots and named the company the Bayou Fund LLC (Bayou).

Family connections and an advertised conservative investment approach brought Israel and his partners, Daniel Marino (chief financial officer) and James Marquez (co-founder),[5] hundreds of investors, and eventually more than $400 million in investments. It helped that the minimum investment in Bayou was $250,000 instead of the $1 million minimum that most hedge funds insist upon. Bayou reported steady profits of between 10 and 15 percent.

Israel and his partners quickly learned that they were no good at picking stocks. In 1997, faced with the prospect of sending out monthly statements that revealed their ineptitude, the three decided instead to fire their independent auditor and manufacture phony statements showing a modest gain, hoping that they could make up the losses later on. Needing an auditor to certify the accuracy of numbers that were *not* accurate, the three created a phony accounting firm called Richmond-Fairfield Associates with an address (but not a working office) on Madison Avenue in New York City. As a CPA, Marino led the accounting fraud.

Continuing to report false, steady returns of between 10 and 15 percent per year brought Bayou hundreds of millions of dollars in new investments from pension funds, other hedge funds, and university endowments. Israel and Marino used that money to pay distributions to earlier investors and to fund lifestyles befitting their phony station. But continued poor performance made them desperate for large returns. That desperation eventually led them into the hands of a long con scamster running a prime bank fraud. Israel wired the scamster $100 million,[6] and the Bayou snowball picked up speed on its path downhill.

Meanwhile, according to the SEC, investment adviser Hennessee Group LLC (Hennessee), a prominent New York investment adviser, was recommending that its clients invest in Bayou. Its clients felt comfortable doing so because Hennessee touted its supposed extensive due diligence of every fund that it recommended. For example, Hennessee client DePauw University invested more than $3 million of its endowment in Bayou on Hennessee's recommendation.

DePauw and Bayou's other investors were surprised when, in the summer of 2005, they received a letter from Israel saying that he was closing Bayou to spend more time with his family and that checks representing the balance of investors' accounts were in the mail. Prompted by a bounced check for $53 million, one Bayou client traveled from Seattle to Bayou's offices in Stamford, Connecticut, only to find them empty. On Dan Marino's desk, the investor found a purported suicide letter detailing how Bayou had been a fraud almost from its inception. News traveled fast, prompting Israel to drive from his stone mansion in Mount Kisco, New York—rented from Donald Trump for $32,000 per month—to the U.S. attorney's office in Manhattan to turn himself in.

Israel, Marino, and Marquez all pleaded guilty to the charges related to Bayou, no doubt hoping for light, white-collar sentences.

At his sentencing hearing, in a courtroom packed with his victims, Israel spent more time whining about the pressures of living up to his family's expectations than he did apologizing. U.S. District Judge Colleen McMahon was not moved. She sentenced Israel to 20 years in prison but allowed him 60 days to put his affairs in order.[7] Judge McMahon ordered Israel to report to federal prison in Ayer, Massachusetts, no later than 2 p.m. on June 9, 2008, to begin serving his sentence. At about 10 a.m. that day, Israel parked his SUV on the Bear Mountain Bridge.

As Israel was scrawling his suicide note on the hood of his SUV, his girlfriend, Debra Ryan, pulled alongside, and Israel got into her car. They drove to an RV parked nearby that the two had packed full of supplies the day before. Israel drove the RV just over 110 miles that day, arriving at the Prospect Mountain Campground in Granville, Massachusetts, at about the time he should have been reporting to the Federal Correctional Center at Ayer, Massachusetts, another two hours farther northeast. He registered under the name David Klapp and spent the rest of June there.

Finding no body floating in the Hudson, federal authorities told the Customs Service to look out for Israel, possibly traveling with a false passport. The FBI interviewed Ryan. After days of repeating the cover story that she and Israel had agreed upon, she admitted the hoax and was arrested. When news of his disappearance and Ryan's arrest hit *America's Most Wanted*, Israel came out of hiding. He took the Yamaha scooter off the back of the RV and rode to the police station in Southwick, Massachusetts, where he gave himself up. With two years added to his sentence for his escape attempt, Israel will now leave prison in August 2027 at age 68, maybe a couple of years earlier if he behaves himself.[8]

The SEC ultimately charged Hennessee with making misrepresentations to its clients about the supposedly thorough due diligence it had performed on Bayou. Hennessee settled the case without admitting or denying the SEC's allegations.

Had Hennessee done the due diligence that it had promised to do, it would have found several troubling red flags flying over Israel and Bayou. Israel did not graduate from Tulane, although he led people to believe that he had. He also exaggerated his responsibilities at his pre-Bayou employers. And a former employee had sued Bayou in 2003, alleging that Israel had fired him for pointing out bookkeeping irregularities at Bayou.

While some of those revelations seem rather minor, the vigilant investor understands that there is no such thing as a "white" lie from someone with access to her nest egg. Hedge fund investors are betting their entire investment on the integrity and skill of the manager. Any misrepresentation of the manager's background reveals a willingness to withhold bad news, the very thing that strikes the spark for most hedge fund conflagrations.

Hennessee is not alone in its due diligence lapses, and the SEC's case against it highlights a continuing danger to funds-of-funds investors. Investment advisers routinely promise to do stringent due diligence, but they rarely do everything that they promise. In the course of an investigation of a hedge fund adviser for an Investor's Watchdog client, we noted that the New York–based adviser charged a 1 percent fee for "initial and continuing due diligence" on alternative investments. Given the adviser's assets under management, that fee would have created a fund of more than $2 million for due diligence investigation each year. Yet we found that this investment adviser had led his clients into Bernard Madoff's funds. A fraction of the $2 million per year that was supposed to be in the due diligence fund would have been sufficient to uncover enough evidence to warn investors away from Madoff, Bayou, and any other operating hedge fund fraud.

Because they are not trained at recognizing the warning signs of fraud, and because they operate under an undiagnosed congruence bias, fund managers, especially funds-of-funds managers, routinely miss red flags that you can spot if you are on your guard. The congruence bias is even more dangerous when, as is typical, the adviser who directs investors to the fund receives a fee from the hedge fund for each investment.

While fund managers routinely disclose the conflict of interest created by their receipt of referral fees, the vigilant investor understands that just because an adviser admits a possible conflict of interest does not mean that the adviser is not influenced by that conflict. The whole idea behind requiring investment advisers to disclose conflicts of interest is so that investors can avoid those advisers. Yet most investors read right over the conflict disclosure and may even credit the adviser with scrupulous honesty for admitting a conflict. Consider a *possible* conflict to be an *actual* conflict and choose investment advisers who get an independent investigation of all funds in which they invest. Ask your adviser to identify the person who performs the due diligence investigations and learn whether he has experience in uncovering fraud or only experience in evaluating the likely profitability of investments. The approach makes all the difference.

Like most hedge fund frauds, Bayou targeted pension funds, endowments, and very wealthy individuals. But, as evidenced by Bayou's lower minimum investment, it also targeted retirees who might have the minimum investment in a self-directed IRA or other nest egg account.

Under federal securities laws, only investors who meet the definition of an *accredited investor* are allowed to invest in unregistered investments like hedge funds. Under the rules passed as part of the Dodd-Frank Act, a person is considered accredited if he (1) has $200,000 in annual income (or $300,000 jointly with a spouse) in each of the past two years and expects to have at least that much income in the current year, or (2) has a net worth of $1 million, excluding the value of the investor's primary residence.

The theory behind restricting hedge fund investments to accredited investors is that investors with that amount of income or net worth are sophisticated enough to fully comprehend the risks associated with alternative investments and/or have the wherewithal to suffer a large loss. But, as Benjamin Franklin said, "There is nothing more horrible in nature as to see a beautiful theory murdered by an ugly gang of facts." Many accredited investors rely on investment advisers to vet potential investments, surrendering their theoretical sophistication to the judgment of their investment adviser. When the adviser gets money for directing a client to a particular fund, any objectivity that she may have had vanishes, and no one stands between the investor and financial ruin.

Whether a pension fund or an elderly retiree, what leads many investors into a hedge fund fraud is the age-old drive to keep up with the Joneses. That desire builds when the stock market is running, approaching new highs, and the press is full of stories about the fantastic returns that some traders are earning. The investor looks at his account and starts to pine for bigger returns.

Every investor who chases returns is susceptible to hedge fund fraud, because hedge fund fraudsters can show attractive returns. Rather than focusing on whether you are keeping pace with the profits that the hottest traders are earning, focus on what you want your nest egg to do (provide for expected living expenses in retirement, pass a certain amount on to the next generation, and so on) and how to reach those goals while minimizing the risk of a catastrophic loss. After all, unless the latest hot trader is going to include you in his will, what does his trading have to do with you, really? Like a dog that chases cars, those who constantly chase returns often wind up flattened.

The vigilant investor stays away from alternative investments that use an affiliated broker to execute trades and investigates to determine whether supposedly independent brokers and auditors are truly independent. Bayou traded through Bayou Securities and Madoff through Madoff Securities not to save on trading costs, but to control access to the information that would have revealed their frauds sooner. Bayou created Richmond-Fairfield Associates out of whole cloth as a supposedly independent auditor. Had an investor investigated Richmond-Fairfield, either in person or by sending an investigator to its offices and interviewing the people there, that one visit would have ended the Bayou fraud on the spot, saving the nest eggs of everyone who gave Bayou money from 1997 to 2005.

Although they target accredited investors and institutional investors, hedge fund frauds also reach investors who are not accredited when scamsters simply ignore the rules about accredited investors. Certainly, most investors have neither an understanding of the accredited investor definition nor an appreciation of how it is designed to protect them. There is no shortage of scamsters who simply ignore the securities laws altogether, raising money from the more than 99 percent of the population who are not trained in what the securities laws require of those who sell investments.

The Scam Mall

Imagine that you are a financial scam artist. How do you decrease the risk that a prospective mark will say no? What many scam artists do is package the same scam in several different ways to look like distinct financial products, each designed to appeal to a certain type of investor. "Not looking for a long-term investment right now? I understand. We also have midrange and short-term investments." We call this kind of operation a *scam mall* because there seems to be something for everyone.

In April 2009, the SEC found a scam mall operating next door to Disneyland at the Desert Palms Hotel and Suites in Anaheim, California. Through seminars held at that hotel, Sun Empire and Empire Capital Asset Management (ECAM) offered three different iterations of the same fraud. One description of the product promised that in exchange for an investment of $4,995 the investor would receive $35,000 per month. But ECAM also dressed up the scam in two other disguises to make it easier to sell to everyone. If the defendants were trying to sell to parents of young children, ECAM offered the "College Advantage Program," under which parents of children between 12 months and 9 years old invested $5,000 and received a guarantee that they would receive no less than $1 million by the time their child reached college. For senior citizens who were more interested in safety than growth, the defendants offered investments styled as certificates of deposit earning 5 to 10 times more than the rates available at banks. ECAM raised more than $9 million.

Scam malls often target people who have been involved with multilevel marketing programs. Like Amway, these programs promise to compensate the seller not only for his own sales, but also for the sales of others whom he recruits to the program. Like those programs, the scam mall will offer you the opportunity to join the sales force and thus earn a commission on sales that you make to others.

Scam mall operators will pay you a percentage of every sale you make and encourage you to tell your family and friends about their products. They will often roll out new products when sales of the existing offerings begin to flag. They will almost always allow investors to pay by credit card. In the days before the credit crunch, it was common for scam mall operators to encourage marks to take out credit card cash advances to invest more in the program, promising to pay a monthly distribution of much more than the interest expense on the loan from Visa. Of course, when the SEC, the FTC, or a state regulator exposes the scam, any payments from the scam stop, but the credit card bills remain, and the victims sink to a level of desperation in which they long for the days when their financial outlook was merely bleak.

Despite ECAM's seemingly ridiculous promises, do not get the impression that the scam mall is easy to spot. Operators will use part of the money that they raise to hire staff members and set up an administrative operation to advance the illusion of legitimacy. In my first receivership assignment, we found an office staffed with five full-time employees whose job was to get investors to fill out paperwork and send in copies of their mortgage documents, credit card statements, and driver's licenses. Those documents had absolutely nothing to do with any investment. They were simply a part of the illusion. "If they need these documents," investors were expected to think, "there must be something real going on." The scamster did not need the documents, but it had an office of people whose task was to demand them and file them correctly.

Scam malls tend to prey on middle-class investors, relying heavily on the kind of high-energy presentations that you might get from a television pitchman. Notice the $4,995 cost of the investment in the ECAM case. You can almost hear a television pitchman screaming, "Only forty-nine ninety-five! But wait! If you invest now, we'll throw in a guaranteed bankruptcy filing!"

When you ask a scam mall operator how she generates the fantastic return, the description of the supposed profit-generating engine may sound very much like a prime bank scam. It will usually involve an overseas component. Like Sam Israel and the operators of the Coadum scam, many scam mall operators have been taken in by prime bank scam operators. Convinced that the trading program is real, they set about raising enough money to meet the supposed minimum investment for entry into the trading program. By asking for every detail of how the investment generates the return, you can recognize the hallmarks of a prime bank scam.

In addition to the tools already identified—background checks, assessment of whether the profit-generating plan makes economic sense, and so on—you can recognize a scam mall by the sales methods it uses. Meetings in hotel conference rooms are very big with scam mall operators. They will have impressive PowerPoint presentations, and the pitch will have the feel of a motivational speech.

The vigilant investor asks the person selling the securities whether the securities are registered with the SEC. (Unless there is a specific exemption available, the law requires registration.) If they are, you will be able to view the registration documents on the SEC's web site. Use the search function to find the registration documents and review them carefully. They will contain a thorough biography of the people behind the investment. Beyond what you find there, you can use PACER and state courthouse records searches to find complaints from previous investors and use the National Student Clearinghouse to find out whether the promoter has the degrees that he brags about in the registration documents.

If the salesperson says that the securities are exempt from registration, but the investor is not an accredited investor, call the SEC and state securities regulators to report an unregistered offering. The sooner you call, the more nest eggs you will save.

The Recovery Scam

The hyenas are never far behind the lion. In the winter of 2008, hundreds of people who thought they had a lot in common with Bill Gates suddenly found that they had more in common with the millions of Americans who were facing foreclosure. These were the victims of Bernard Madoff's record-setting $40 billion, three-decade-long Ponzi scheme. Like all scam victims, Madoff's victims looked in vain for any sign of recovery, while scrambling to find a way to support themselves.

On March 10, 2010, as if waking from a long nightmare, Madoff's victims learned that the International Security Investor Protection Corporation (ISIPC), working with Interpol, had found $1.3 billion in Madoff assets tucked away in Malaysia. On its web site, ISIPC posted a photo of a neatly stacked mountain of cash, 40 stacks long, 15 stacks wide, and 20 stacks high, with other photos showing similar piles of cash tucked away in closets. ISIPC posted a quote from Irving Picard, the trustee in charge of gathering assets for eventual return to victims, stating that he had secured approval from the ISIPC office in Switzerland to work with ISIPC in the United States to return the assets to investors. The web site included quotes from Malaysian government officials assuring victims that the Bank of Malaysia was cooperating to arrange wire transfers to the victims. ISIPC asked those claiming a right to recover Madoff assets to forward their contact information, to be checked against a list provided by the Madoff trustee.

There is no legitimate organization called ISIPC. It popped fully formed from the imagination of a scam artist designing what we call a *recovery scam*. The scamsters designed a logo that closely resembled the logo of the Securities Investor Protection Corporation (SIPC), a legitimate U.S. organization that seeks to refund the assets of those who lose money when a brokerage firm closes. ISIPC worked hard to give its web site the same feel as the SIPC web site. By (falsely) quoting Mr. Picard, whose name every Madoff victim knew, and providing links to government web sites, the scamsters made the ISIPC look legitimate, giving their scam the best shot at success.

Recovery scams prey only on those who have already lost money to a scam. They often claim to be government agencies or to have been contracted by the government to assist in the recovery effort. They collect information from the victims and assure them that recovery will be forthcoming shortly. Eventually, the scamsters explain that there is a fee or a tax associated with returning the money from overseas and that the fee or tax must be paid in advance of the transfer. Already desperate investors often scrape together or borrow the money demanded by the scamsters, never to see it again.

Recovery scams follow high-profile cons like remora follow sharks. The United Kingdom's Serious Fraud Office (SFO) has recently warned of a recovery scam allegedly operating through a well-known Canadian law firm that is supposedly pursuing class action claims against British broker-dealers. Scam victims need only contribute their small portion of the legal fees to receive their share of the recovery. The SFO warned investors that the Canadian law firm has never heard of the "attorneys" who are calling prospective investors soliciting for class action clients. Just like the SFO, you can unmask a recovery scamster by calling the legitimate enterprise that the salesperson claims employs her.

The vigilant investor will never be the target of a recovery scam, but his friends or family might. You can help those you love avoid this insult after injury by warning them in advance that recovery scamsters are never far behind the revelation of a scam and by offering to help investigate any offers to assist in recovery. A simple telephone call to the regulator who pursued the original scam will unmask a recovery scam. In the ISIPC case, the SEC quickly issued a press release warning Madoff victims.

The Giveaway

How can it be a scam if they haven't asked me for any money and haven't asked for my social security number, bank account number, or credit card number? Famous last words.

A scam that prospers in difficult economic times is one that we call the *giveaway*. Usually through a friend or family member, people hear of a humanitarian organization that is giving away money or free debit cards worth $50 per week to everyone who signs up. The organization is supposedly motivated by the plight of the working poor the world over and is committed to creating a new economic paradigm. It has trillions in assets and is set to begin making payments to members of the organization in a matter of weeks or months.

There is no obligation, you are told, and all the organization needs is your name and contact information. It does not ask for your social security number. It does not want your date of birth, your mother's maiden name, the name of your childhood pet, or your bank account information. All it asks for is "information that anyone could get off the Internet anyway." What's the harm?

I have been monitoring the comments on a blog post I wrote more than three years ago about a potential giveaway scam. The conversation between those who believe that the program is legitimate and those who believe that it is a scam has become quite heated. Those who believe in the program call the other side cynical. The skeptics are more forgiving, but just as vociferously call the believers suckers.

It is hard to know how many people have signed up for membership in this organization. Estimates so far put the number above 100,000. It has been more than four years since those behind the program first promised that the money was beginning to flow. But four years of waiting has not dimmed the hopes of those who truly believe. They expect the gates to vast riches to swing wide any day now.

Unless you know what comes next, it is hard to argue with the logic of those who fall for this scam. Having been asked for nothing more than information available from anywho.com, those who want to believe in the giveaway argue, "How could it possibly be a scam?" The true believer never gets a satisfactory answer to that question and spends countless hours daydreaming about how he will finally be able to pay his rent on time and maybe even be able to afford a house. He tells his friends and family about the program and encourages them to sign up to receive the free money.

At roughly 120 million to 1, your odds of winning the lottery are better than your odds of receiving money from a giveaway scam. When the operators of the program decide that they have signed up as many members as possible, they will put out the exciting news that they are now only days away from unlocking the vast wealth of the program. They just need to get permits from the European Union, or file certain required regulatory documents, or prepay certain taxes or legal fees, and the money will then start to flow. Because the wealth is locked up overseas, though, they have to raise the funds to pay those fees or put those tax payments in escrow. Luckily, because of the size of their organization, they need only $250 from each member. Because that is pocket change compared with what each member will receive once the vault is open, this is an easy call for most members. They send in their $250. Thereafter, they will get e-mails updating them on how their money is being spent. But the vault will remain closed. They may get another e-mail filling them in on a small bump in the road that will require another $150 per member. Having already spent $250, each member will dutifully send in another $150, and another $100 when the third solicitation comes.

You've guessed it by now: There is no treasure. There is only a two-stage scam that often takes years to set up, but pays off quite handsomely for the scam operators in the end. If the scam operators have convinced 200,000 people to become members and each one sends in a total of $500, the scam artists will make off with $100 million. But even if a particular investor does not respond to the second-stage solicitation, by giving the supposed philanthropists her contact information, she has helped the scam artists.

Like every salesperson, scam artists need to identify marks who are likely to invest. One of the more valuable lists is that of people who respond to the first stage of a giveaway scam. By providing their contact information, those people identify themselves as people who are willing to believe a fantastic story, and no one is better at spinning fantastic stories than a scam artist. The giveaway scam therefore gives the scam artist what theater and movie fans can think of as the Glengarry leads.[9]

The vigilant investor knows that a promise of something for nothing is always followed by a request for something. Don't waste your time wondering, *What if it's true?* Instead, warn others away from an apparent giveaway scam.

Due Diligence for the Vigilant

The vigilant investor:

► Knows that he is bright enough to understand any legitimate investment, and refuses to invest in anything that he does not understand

► Understands that there is no such thing as a "white" lie from someone who has access to her nest egg

► Considers a *possible* conflict of interest to be an *actual* conflict and favors investment advisers who get a vigilant, independent investigation of all funds in which they invest

► Does not chase returns to keep up with the investment Joneses, but focuses on achieving his own goals while minimizing the risk of a fraud loss

► Avoids alternative investments that use an affiliated broker to execute trades, and investigates whether supposedly independent brokers and auditors are real and are truly independent

► Questions investment promoters on the specifics of how the investment earns profits, in order to draw out any hints of a long con in progress

► Avoids investments that allow payment by credit card

► Avoids investments that encourage investors to recruit their friends and family

4

The Phantom Factory and the Origami Airline

Offering Frauds, Pump and Dumps, and
Why You Can't Believe Your Eyes

All warfare is based on deception.

—Sun Tzu

Newtown, Bucks County, Pennsylvania, is a quaint Philadelphia suburb across the Delaware River from Trenton, New Jersey. In 1995,
YBM Magnex International, Inc. (YBM), an international manufac-
turer of industrial magnets, selected Newtown as its worldwide headquarters.

YBM was a publicly traded company whose shares traded on the
Toronto Stock Exchange. In 1997, it applied unsuccessfully for listing

on U.S. stock exchanges. While this would have made the company's shares only marginally more accessible,[1] the company craved the prestige and implicit stamp of legitimacy that trading on these exchanges would bring.

With former Ontario Premier David Peterson on its board of directors, YBM became the darling of the Toronto Exchange. Coopers & Lybrand had previously done accounting work for the company, and Deloitte & Touche was currently retained. In filings with Canadian securities regulators, YBM reported revenues of hundreds of millions of dollars from the manufacture and sale of magnets. It issued press releases about its success and held investor conferences at which it touted the company's profitability. Shares in YBM rose from $0.10 per share[2] in July 1994 to $20.15 per share in March 1998.

By 1998, however, the SEC and the Department of Justice had begun to smell a rat; they received a tip that YBM had (unsuccessfully) offered its auditors a $500,000 bribe to certify the accuracy of the company's financial statements. When the FBI raided YBM's headquarters, it found bank statements, invoices, and purchase orders for millions of dollars in magnet sales, and thousands of pages of additional documents related to the profitable business, but no magnets.

While hedge fund and investment limited partnership fraudsters claim to earn profits by trading baskets of investments—from stocks and bonds to real estate and mortgage-backed securities—some frauds, like YBM, claim to earn returns that are tied directly to the success of a business enterprise. We call these *offering frauds* because the fraudsters "offer" either equity in or debt backed by the company. In this chapter, we will examine several offering frauds and explain how the vigilant investor can recognize and avoid them.

The Brainy Don and the Phantom Factory

YBM was the work of Russian mobster Simeon Mogilevich. Mogilevich grew up near Kiev, Ukraine, the son of middle-class parents. He graduated from the University of Lviv at the age of 22 with a degree in economics, but he fell in with criminal gangs and began supporting himself with petty crimes. Those crimes led to two stints in Siberian prisons, where he met established mobsters who supplemented his formal education with a criminal education. When he left prison, Mogilevich quickly built his own criminal enterprise, profiting from prostitution, extortion, drug smuggling, arms trafficking, money laundering, and even the sale of nuclear weapons materials.

Mogilevich has all the trappings of a successful international businessman. He speaks several languages; holds passports from Russia, the Ukraine, Israel, and Hungary; and even owns interests in several legitimate businesses. But beneath the veneer of legitimacy, he is the boss of all Russian mob bosses, the *capo di tutti capi*. American, Russian, and European police agencies consider him the most dangerous Russian mobster alive. He is now sharing space with Osama bin Laden on the FBI's Ten Most Wanted list, and his combination of education, business acumen, and ruthlessness has earned him the nickname "the Brainy Don."

Mogilevich ran his YBM scam from his home in Budapest, providing $2.4 million in seed money to create the business. He bribed lawyers and accountants to set up a network of shell companies to disguise his ownership of YBM, to make the enterprise look legitimate, and to gain approval for shares in YBM to trade on the Toronto Stock Exchange. When he sold his shares, he reaped a profit of $18.4 million, leaving purchasers of the shares holding an ownership interest in a phantom enterprise. While he was arrested in Moscow in 2008 on relatively minor tax evasion charges, Mogilevich's widespread bribery of government officials makes it unlikely that he will ever spend a significant amount of time in prison. Because there is no extradition treaty between Russia and the United States, it is highly unlikely that he will ever have to answer for his YBM fraud.

Mogilevich's YBM was a *pump-and-dump* scam writ large. Before we look at the basics of a pump-and-dump scam, though, let's consider how a vigilant investor might have spotted and avoided investing in a scheme as sophisticated as YBM.

Avoiding the YBM scam would have been difficult under any circumstances because it was so well disguised. For the reasons we discussed in Chapter 1, investors tend to believe that any company that can attract a former prominent member of the Canadian government to its board of directors, convince two of the big four international accounting firms to do its accounting work, and have its shares listed on the Toronto Stock Exchange must be legitimate. So how could an investor have known otherwise?

One clue was that YBM was never able to gain listing on an American stock exchange. Although Canadian authorities work hard to prevent it, many offering fraudsters begin their scams on Canadian exchanges. Unlike the United States, Canada has no federal securities enforcer comparable to the SEC. Instead, each Canadian province and territory has its own securities enforcement agency. A lack of communication between law enforcement agencies can have disastrous consequences, and in the absence of a single federal securities regulator in Canada, the chance of that kind of lapse in communication is increased. That may explain why offering frauds tend to thrive on Canadian exchanges more than on American exchanges. A savvy investor approaches an investment in a business that trades only on a

Canadian exchange with an appreciation of that increased risk. In the YBM case, a vigilant investor would have been doubly suspicious of a U.S.-based company that could not gain listing on a U.S. exchange.

A vigilant investor would also have noticed that YBM had changed accountants. Publicly traded companies don't change accountants often; it is expensive for a new accounting firm to bring itself up to speed on the financial operations of a worldwide company. You must question why a company would agree to spend that much money. Sometimes the reason is that the current accountant has found financial irregularities and refuses to certify the company's financial statements. Rather than risk disclosure of that refusal, the company will fire this firm and go fishing for one that will sign off on the company's financial statements. Note that both Deloitte & Touche and Coopers & Lybrand refused to sign off on YBM's financial statements.

Companies that trade on U.S. exchanges must file a Form 8-K with the SEC when they change accountants. A search through a company's public filings on the SEC web site will uncover any 8-Ks. Other events can trigger an 8-K filing as well,[3] all of them significant. You therefore should peruse the 8-K filings of any company in which you plan to invest. Investors in companies that are listed only on Canadian exchanges should reread the first 12 paragraphs of this chapter.

The Pump and Dump

One of the reasons that the YBM scam was so difficult to spot was that it made the Toronto Exchange an unwitting accomplice. Every pump-and-dump scam does so. The tactic works because even the most skeptical investor does not appreciate how a scamster can manipulate the data reported by a stock exchange. It's actually pretty easy, and it's essential to the pump phase of the pump and dump.

The central challenge in any pump-and-dump scam is pumping up, or creating, a demand for worthless stock that the scamster owns or controls. Stocks, like other goods and services, obey the law of supply and demand. The greater the demand for a stock, the higher the price. Whether it's stocks or goods that you sell on eBay, you make people want something (1) by making it seem valuable and/or (2) by making them think that other people want it. Pump-and-dump scamsters use both approaches.

Pump-and-dump scamsters make people think that the worthless stock is valuable by issuing false press releases detailing supposedly wonderful developments at the company. At YBM, press releases claimed millions of dollars in revenue from new business through contracts to build industrial magnets.

Most investors don't realize how easy it is to issue a press release. It involves nothing more than drafting the text and paying to have it issued on a commercial newswire. The word *press* in the term *press release* does not mean that Anderson Cooper is interested in the company.

In addition to issuing false press releases, pump-and-dump scamsters create the impression that their stock is in great demand by manipulating the data reported by the stock exchange. They do this by giving several thousand shares to their criminal cohorts and directing them to trade it back and forth among themselves several times per day at gradually increasing prices. The scamster thus pumps up the volume reported by the stock exchange without ever losing control of a single share.

When interested investors do their research, they see positive developments at the company, a steady rise in the stock price, and so many shares traded that it seems as if everyone thinks that owning shares is a good idea. The pump-and-dump scamster increases demand further by paying affiliated stockbrokers to recommend the stock to their customers. Once these efforts create enough demand to lift the stock to a predetermined price, the cohorts stop selling shares to one another and instead sell the scamster's shares to innocent buyers. All at once the press releases stop; the phony volume dries up; and, since no one else is interested in buying the shares, the innocent investors watch the price of the stock drop like the popularity of disco. The scam artist and his cohorts move on to the next pump-and-dump scheme while the bewildered investors calculate their losses.

The SEC will commence enforcement actions against dozens of pump-and-dump schemes this year. These scams are a lucrative business with a strong track record of easy money. A vigilant investor avoids them by understanding that press releases don't always tell the truth, and that scamsters can manipulate price and volume data. When a broker calls you up with a breathless pitch for a hot stock, listen closely, and if the broker mentions press releases, increasing volume, and a steadily rising stock price during the pitch, insist on doing more investigation.

The Origami Airline

Music runs in Lou Pearlman's family; he is Art Garfunkel's first cousin. It was perhaps natural, then, that Pearlman made a fortune as the mastermind behind the boy bands *NSYNC and Backstreet Boys in the 1990s. But Pearlman also had interests beyond the music industry.

Pearlman created Trans Continental Airlines, Inc., in the 1980s, positioning the company as a charter airline service in a notoriously tough industry. Its operations were impressive enough to convince a large German bank, Deutschland Invest und Finanzberatung (DIF), to take a major stake. Trans Continental's balance sheet, audited by Coral Gables, Florida, accounting firm Cohen & Siegel, was impressive enough to convince the likes of Bank of America and Washington Mutual to extend $150 million in credit. Those banks and the hundreds of investors who invested in Trans Continental discovered in 2006 that Trans Continental was flying paper airplanes. The entire company was a creation of Lou Pearlman's imagination.

You can imagine how DIF reacted upon learning that its stake in Pearlman's airline was worthless. Actually, DIF did not take the news badly, because DIF never existed. Like the airline, the big German bank that showed such faith in Pearlman was a creation of Pearlman's imagination. In fact, on June 14, 2007, when the U.S. marshals caught up with Pearlman—registered at a hotel in Bali under the name A. Incognito Johnson—he was on a mission to have someone create a phony corporate seal and other corporate documents vouching for the existence of the phony German bank.

Imagine being the partners at accounting firm Cohen & Siegel upon finding out about a fraud of this magnitude. If you know anyone who worked for Arthur Andersen in the days following the Enron collapse, you can appreciate the blood pressure spike that comes with finding out that you have certified the accuracy of fictitious financial statements. You check your malpractice policy and wonder whether the civil judgments against you will exceed your coverage, and you start dusting off your résumé. You get a lawyer and wonder whether you will have to plead the Fifth Amendment in an effort to avoid jail time.

But neither Cohen nor Siegel let Pearlman's fraud cause him a moment of anxiety, because neither of them ever existed, either. There never was an accounting firm called Cohen & Siegel. There never were any audits. There never were any real financial statements to audit. Pearlman covered all of his bases, and the investors in his airline, from Bank of America and Washington Mutual right down to the mom-and-pop investors who gave Pearlman their nest eggs, lost more than $400 million.

Lou Pearlman is now known as prisoner number 02775-093 in the Federal Correctional Institution in Texarkana, Texas. He gets out in 2029. While vigilante investors may be waiting for him when he walks out, the vigilant investor never would have invested in Pearlman's airline.

Of course, an investigation sufficient to uncover the three layers of Pearlman's fraud might have required travel, but not beyond the offices of Cohen & Siegel. Had an investor arrived at the offices of Cohen & Siegel, he would have found only an answering service that forwarded Cohen & Siegel mail to Pearlman's Orlando office.

The kind of phony accounting con that was so important to Pearlman's scam—and to Sam Israel's Bayou scam, for that matter—can be a phantom operation, as it was in Pearlman's case. But other scam artists might give the name and address of an actual accounting firm, so that an investor who does nothing more than drive by the address will be comforted. Of course, no one inside that office would have ever heard of the company that the firm supposedly audited. Finding that out would require going inside.

In the most extreme case, where the scamster has created an office equipped with actors to play the role of accounting professionals, a few questions and follow-up investigation by a vigilant investor can unmask the scamster.[4] First, always arrive unannounced. Criminal cohorts are always prepared when they know they can expect a visit from a mark. Then explain that you are considering a substantial investment in the company and are doing your due diligence. Ask to speak to a CPA, preferably one of the partners. If the CPA refuses to be interviewed, offer to call the CEO via speakerphone and get his permission for the accountant to answer your questions. In the guise of small talk, you should be able to find out where the accountant went to school, when she graduated, and when she was licensed as a CPA. Look at any diplomas on the wall of the accountant's office, and make note of the schools and the dates on the diplomas. Notice the absence of any. Ask open-ended questions: "What can you tell me about the company?" "What can you tell me about the CEO of the company?" "What is his background?" "What are the primary assets and liabilities of the company?" Ask how long the accountant has been auditing the company's books.

Of course, finding an empty office, a group of accountants who have never heard of your scam artist, or an answering service will tell you all you need to know. If the scamster was hyperprepared, it is time to check the information that you received from your interview with possible criminal cohorts. Call your state's board of accountancy. Ask for the year in which the CPA was licensed, her business address, and any information about disciplinary actions. If Lou Pearlman had arranged for someone to play the role of Mr. Cohen or Mr. Siegel, a call to the accountancy board would have revealed that no such accounting business was licensed in the state. Check the information about education with the National Student Clearinghouse, and remember, there are no white lies. Finally, pay attention to that bad feeling that you got when you spoke to the "accountant."

A vigilant investor who was considering entrusting money to Trans Continental would have looked further into DIF because Pearlman touted its stake in the airline. While a trip to Germany is beyond the investigative budget for most investors—although institutional investors would want to make that trip rather than make a several-million-dollar mistake—investigating overseas does not always require traveling overseas. Google Maps can help confirm whether a business exists at the location listed on its web site. In one of our Investor's Watchdog assignments, our suspicions of fraud were aroused when Google Maps showed us that the supposed headquarters of the business was actually a parking garage in the City of London.

Even neighboring businesses can help. A Google search for the supposed address of the overseas business will yield the names of businesses in the same building or on the same street. Call them. If you ask nicely and explain that you are considering an important investment in the company, they will even take the elevator up or down a few floors or walk around the corner on their lunch hour to be your eyes and ears halfway around the world. Is there a business there? What is the name on the sign on the door? How many people work there? These questions and others can confirm or refute the representations of the person who promises to grow your life savings.

Ideally, you will visit the supposedly thriving business, but there is danger here. The best-prepared scam artists love nothing better than to give a tour of their thriving business and demonstrate its profit making in action.

Don't Believe Your Eyes

According to the Royal Canadian Mounted Police (RCMP), Gary Sorenson and Milowe Brost went to that kind of trouble in the course of an offering fraud that bilked thousands of people across the globe out of their retirement nest eggs. Sorenson and Brost lured people into investing in a company that they called Syndicated Gold Depository, S.A. (SGD), which was supposed to loan money to a gold-mining operation called Merendon Mining Corp. Ltd. at interest rates that would provide a healthy return for investors. Unbeknownst to the victims, there never were any significant gold-mining operations.

The SGD scam operated for almost 10 years, from 1999 to 2008, defrauding more than 3,000 victims out of more than $300 million. At the suggestion of the SGD sales team, many investors borrowed against their home equity to get the cash to invest in SGD, which promised returns of between 18 and 36 percent annually and represented that the loans were fully collateralized by gold. Sorenson hosted tours for potential investors at a Honduran refinery and demonstrated the pouring of gold bars while making false claims about the profitability of his company. You can imagine the investors' reaction: "I actually saw them pouring gold bars!"

Scam artists are eager to set up operations that mimic a legitimate business because no one believes anything as much as what he sees with his own eyes. Many years ago, I represented people who invested in a company that claimed to have vast coal deposits. There were meetings in the woods of Kentucky, and the investors saw the seams of coal. But it was a fraud nonetheless. The coal was of poor quality, and the costs of removing it were prohibitive.

The pouring of the gold bars in the SGD scam was a stunt. Whether SGD had anything to do with the place at which the investors supposedly witnessed the gold bars being poured is unclear. But even assuming that it did, does the pouring of a gold bar or seeing visible seams of coal mean that the investment promoter will use your money for legitimate business operations?

The vigilant investor thinks of a visit to the business as an opportunity to find a reason *not* to invest, rather than an opportunity to confirm the legitimacy of the entire enterprise. Of course, a surprise visit is always better than a visit arranged by the investment promoter.

Enron, the former American energy company, understood the power of visual evidence. Having created the company in 1985 out of the merger of two existing natural gas pipeline companies, CEO Ken Lay began managing its image and its stock price aggressively. On the advice of Chief Operating Officer Jeffrey Skilling and Chief Financial Officer Andrew Fastow, Lay valued Enron's assets aggressively, while hiding many of its substantial liabilities in so-called off-balance sheet transactions conducted through supposedly independent shell companies. Enron bullied its auditor, Arthur Andersen LLP, into going along with this aggressive accounting approach. Stock analysts and the public therefore saw only what Enron wanted them to see.

Among the things that Enron wanted stock analysts to see was its impressive energy-trading room at its Houston headquarters. In 1998, it arranged for analysts who covered the company to witness the profitable trading of energy contracts firsthand with a visit to the trading room. Enron staged the entire scene, setting up computers and giving instructions on what the employees sitting at the computers should do and say while the analysts were in the room. The employees pretended to be trading energy contracts. The analysts bought it. When the analysts left, the charade ended. In 2001, Enron ended.[5]

At its peak, Enron was the seventh largest company in the United States. In 1998, when analysts visited the fake trading room, its stock traded at $22 per share. Thereafter, it peaked at $90 per share in 2000, before falling to worthless after the company filed for Chapter 11 bankruptcy protection in December 2001. The lesson to take from Enron's creation of the fake trading room is that con artists of every stripe—from career con artists to career corporate executives—understand the power of a staged visit to the supposedly profitable business and will use it, if possible, to take your retirement savings from you.

The short-lived fall 2010 Fox TV show *Lone Star*, about a father and son con team, included an effective demonstration of a typical staged site visit. The supposed investment was in an oil and gas operation. When the investor asked to see the operating oil well, the father and son scamsters handled it this way. The son visited an operating well the day before and told the foreman that he was a location scout for a major motion picture that planned on filming in the area and that he would like to bring his director by the next day to observe the location. By slipping the foreman a tip for his help, he ensured that no one would challenge him when he arrived with the mark in tow. On the day of the visit, the father posed as the foreman and explained how profitable the operation was and how they were on the verge of finding oil deposits that would dwarf what they had found so far. I wish the show had made it. It was true to life. Hollywood probably scrapped it for being unbelievable.

Due Diligence for the Vigilant

The vigilant investor:

▶ Is skeptical of American companies whose shares trade only in Canada

▶ Questions why a publicly traded company would incur the substantial expense of changing accountants and investigates whether it's because the former accountant found financial irregularities that the company wants to keep hidden

➤ Reviews 8-K filings for any U.S. companies in which he is considering investing

➤ Never invests solely on the basis of positive press releases, increased trading volume, and rising stock prices

➤ Makes unannounced visits to the business and related professionals and gets answers that can be verified through independent sources

➤ Calls state licensing boards to confirm the identity of supposed professionals

➤ Uses satellite images, Google Maps, and friendly neighbors to test representations about operating offices

5

Affinity Fraud and the Evil Twin

How Someone Who Looks a Lot Like You Is Plotting to Take Your Nest Egg

You cannot serve both God and money.

—JESUS

When clients walked into Frank Castaldi's modest office on Cumberland Avenue in Norridge, Illinois, they often got a friendly kiss on both cheeks. Castaldi was a fixture of the Italian American community in suburban Chicago as the owner of Vitangelo's Pizza and Restaurant and Cumberland Accounting Services. He attended his clients' birthday and anniversary parties and never failed to bring a lavish gift to the weddings of their children or grandchildren. They considered him a friend.

As a tax preparer, Castaldi was in a position to know the financial wherewithal of his clients. They trusted him because he was one of them. He used that knowledge and trust to lead them into investing their retirement savings in promissory notes paying 10 to 15 percent tax-free. Castaldi said that he generated the return by investing their money in FDIC-insured certificates of deposit or in other insured financial instruments. He told them that he had a special relationship with the financial institutions in which he invested, and he personally guaranteed every investment. None of it was true. Castaldi was operating a Ponzi scheme.

Castaldi's scam is what the SEC calls *affinity fraud* and defines as "investment scams that prey upon members of identifiable groups, such as religious or ethnic communities, the elderly, or professional groups." Affinity fraud is not really a separate type of scam—it can take the form of an offering fraud, a hedge fund fraud, a prime bank fraud, or some other type of fraud—so much as it is a description of the modus operandi of the fraudster. Affinity fraudsters use their own membership in a distinct group to build the trust that is essential to the success of the scheme. In this chapter, we will examine affinity frauds run by a *paisan*, a pastor, a *ganif*, a humanitarian, and a radio host. We'll look at common features of affinity frauds, and we'll learn how to recognize and avoid them.

The *Paisan*

Frank Castaldi raised more than $77 million from 473 investors between 1986 and his indictment in 2008. He spent most of that money on payments to earlier investors to keep the illusion alive, and the rest of it on a failed banquet hall business. According to his written plea agreement, he learned the promissory note con from a relative he worked for in high school and college.

When he arrived in a Chicago courtroom for his sentencing on September 15, 2010, Castaldi was expecting leniency from U.S. District Judge John Darrah. After all, by pleading guilty, Castaldi was saving the government the time and expense of a trial. The Justice Department recommended that Judge Darrah sentence Castaldi to 150 months in prison. Judge Darrah rejected that recommendation and instead sentenced him to 276 months, saying, "This is an offense of huge magnitude." Castaldi is now inmate number 40990-424 in the Allenwood Federal Correction Facility near White Deer, Pennsylvania. He is appealing his sentence.

A recent blog comment by one of Castaldi's victims (who posted anonymously) echoes what I have heard from hundreds of scam victims over more than 20 years of investor protection work and illustrates why affinity frauds are so successful.

> [Castaldi] said he wanted to help us out because "we are like family." . . . None of us knew anything about investing money. What do you do, look in the yellow pages for a stranger? No. You go to someone you trust and have known for years. . . . Isn't that the smart thing to do?

Affinity fraudsters try hard to look like their marks. From the investor's perspective, the thinking goes like this: (1) This person is like me. We share the same heritage. I know how he was raised; (2) I would never defraud anyone, much less people who share so much of my story; (3) *Therefore*, this person would never defraud me.

The flaw in the logic is obvious: The conclusion does not necessarily follow from the premises. Remember that anyone who is offering you an investment, however much of your story she shares, is a flawed human being, subject to temptations and driven by motivations that you do not and cannot fully appreciate. As much as you have in common, you cannot know how this person's character was shaped.

Like Castaldi, affinity fraudsters often offer a guarantee, because their victims are often primarily concerned with protecting their principal. Typical guarantees run the gamut from supposed personal assurances by the investment promoter or an interested third party, to FDIC insurance, to supposed nongovernmental insurance policies that pay off in the event of default. The vigilant investigator loves to find these guarantees, because they are such reliable predictors of fraud. Guarantees go with scamsters like peanut butter goes with jelly.

To understand why personal guarantees from the promoter or any other individual are worthless, think about how much that promoter is raising from all investors and consider whether he has the money (forget the mansion; it's mortgaged to the hilt) to make good on every one of those investments in the event of a default. The answer is no.

If the promised guarantee relates to FDIC insurance, remember that the FDIC pays *depositors* in the event of a bank's failure. If you are not the depositor, the FDIC will not pay you. If something other than a bank failure—such as theft by an investment promoter—leads to the loss of your investment, the FDIC will not pay you. Insist that the investment promoter give you the name of the bank that holds the deposits or CDs. Call the bank—at the number you find with an Internet search, not the number the investment promoter gives you—and explain that you are calling to confirm that you are covered by FDIC insurance. Then ask whether it has you listed as a depositor. It won't.

If the promoter claims that an insurance company will pay claims in the event of a default, ask to see the declarations page (dec page) of the policy. That document will list the insurance company, the insured party, the policy number, the effective date of the policy, and the limits of coverage. You'll probably get a forgery, so don't believe what you see. Call the insurance company (*not* the insurance agent whose name and number the promoter gives you) to verify the information on the dec page. Take good notes so that you can share what you learn with the SEC or state regulators.

There *are* contracts that act somewhat like insurance policies on debt obligations. Credit default swaps (CDSs) involve paying a premium to someone who promises to pay the amount of the obligation in the event of a default. If the investment promoter claims to have entered into a CDS arrangement to cover the eventuality of default, ask to see the CDS documentation. No affinity fraudster will actually purchase a CDS, but she will certainly create a convincing forgery. As with any supposed evidence of a written obligation, the paper is only the beginning of the inquiry. Call the other party to the CDS transaction (*not* the name and number that the investment promoter gives you) and ask for details about the terms of the swap. If you learn that the other party never heard of your investment promoter, call the SEC.

The Pastor

"Never sell the facts. Instead, sell warm stewardship and the Lord," former Pastor Vaughn Reeves, Sr., told the salespeople he recruited to sell church bonds. Reeves's company, Alanar, Inc., of Sullivan, Indiana, identified Protestant churches from Michigan to Florida that needed money to build or expand their church buildings but could not get financing from a bank. Alanar helped its church clients sell bonds to raise the money they needed to build or expand. Most of the bond purchasers were members of the church, but sometimes other Christians invested, eager to earn a stable return while helping other believers. The church got the money from the sale of the bonds, and the investors received interest payments until the church paid off the debt, at which time the investors would receive the return of their principal. At least, that's how Reeves said it would work. By having his salespeople open each sales call with a prayer and stress each prospect's "Christian duty" to help the church, Alanar raised more than $120 million from more than 11,000 investors in 150 separate church bond offerings between 1988 and 2005.

Reeves and his sons, Chip, Chris, and Josh, had a taste for luxurious living. They bought two airplanes, took expensive vacations, drove luxury cars, and lived in enormous houses. Soon there was not enough cash to make the interest payments to bondholders, and Reeves began moving cash from the proceeds of one church's bond offering to make interest payments to investors in a separate bond offering. Some churches defaulted on their loans, but Reeves kept that quiet to avoid spooking investors in prospective offerings. Some churches paid off their debt early, triggering Alanar's obligation to return investors' principal. Reeves paid back principal only to investors who attended the church in question. He continued making "interest" (Ponzi) payments to outside investors to avoid having to write a bigger check for the return of principal. In October 2010, Reeves was convicted on nine counts of fraud. In December 2010, he was sentenced to 54 years in prison.

Like the other types of scams we have covered, affinity fraud ranges from purely imaginary investments (Castaldi) to legitimate businesses gone wrong (Alanar). The point that the vigilant investor takes from the Alanar case is that an appeal to his faith is a red flag, regardless of the existence of an operating business.

The North American Securities Administrators Association

(NASAA) estimates that 80,000 people lost more than $2 billion to religious-based affinity fraud between 1998 and 2001. In scams targeting the faithful, the affinity relates to something more significant than common ancestry; at the very least, it relates to a code of conduct that frowns on fraud. When investors meet an investment promoter who shares their faith, they believe that they understand things about that individual's character that they cannot know about someone who does not share their faith. When the promoter promises a certain return and gives a personal guarantee that the investment will deliver as promised, the mark is tempted to believe that she has received a sort of divine blessing on the venture.

Affinity fraud flourishes in Christian churches in part because of what's known as *prosperity theology*, which asserts that God rewards the faithful with material wealth. In its most flagrant form, the pastors who preach it have encouraged financially desperate followers to scrape together their last $1,000 and give it to the church, promising that God will return it many times over by the time the landlord starts eviction proceedings.

You may remember Jim and Tammy Faye Bakker, the hosts of *The PTL Club*, which aired in the 1980s on more than 100 stations nationwide. The Bakkers sold lifetime memberships in the PTL Club for $1,000 apiece. Membership entitled the member to a three-night stay at a luxury hotel at Heritage USA in Fort Mill, South Carolina, then the third largest theme park in the United States. In 1989, Jim Bakker was convicted of mail fraud, wire fraud, and conspiracy for raising twice the amount of money needed to build the hotel and selling more memberships than the hotel could accommodate. Having finally read the Bible cover to cover while in prison, Bakker commented on the prosperity theology that underlay his sales of PTL memberships by saying, "The more I studied the Bible . . . I had to admit that the prosperity message did not line up with the tenor of Scripture."

Religion relates to the soul, which is, or should be, unconcerned with material wealth. Anyone who appeals to your religious faith in pitching an investment is asking you to hammer a nail with an idea. Certainly, an idea can be more powerful than a hammer, but it is the wrong tool for the job. Fraud aimed at religious groups is so virulent and effective that the only safe course is to refuse to consider any investment pitched by even a subtle appeal to your faith. Make it your Eleventh Commandment.

The *Ganif*

Rabbi Chaim Silver of the B'nai Israel synagogue in Norfolk, Virginia, knew Joseph Shereshevsky. When members of his temple asked Rabbi Silver what he thought of Shereshevsky—who went by the nickname Yossi—the rabbi gave what he thought was an accurate positive recommendation. The rabbi would later have reason to regret that; Shereshevsky was a *ganif* (Hebrew for thief).

Shereshevsky had grown up in Brooklyn, the son of a well-respected rabbi. He graduated from high school and attended a yeshiva, gaining an education in Orthodox Jewish law. He worked in New York's diamond district for several years before disputes with business associates led to his arrest and guilty pleas on charges of attempted grand larceny and bank fraud. Avoiding jail time and seeking to put his old life behind him, Shereshevsky moved to Norfolk in 2001, changing his name to Heller. His encyclopedic knowledge of the Talmud and tradition quickly gained him friends in that community. He was invited to join Rabbi Silver's congregation at B'nai Israel, he married a woman from a prominent Orthodox family, and he landed a job working for a rental property management firm. Soon, he received a promotion to seeking out real estate investments for the owner of the rental properties he managed.

In 2003, Shereshevsky met Steven Byers, CEO of Chicago-based WexTrust Capital, Inc., which described itself as a "private equity and specialty finance company specializing in real estate, specialty finance, and investment banking." Touting offices in Chicago, Norfolk, New York, Nashville, Atlanta, Boca Raton, Tel Aviv, and Johannesburg, WexTrust purported to earn profits through buying, renovating, and either selling or operating commercial property, including hotels. Shereshevsky became part owner and the COO of the company. When the time came to raise money for the next WexTrust offering, he offered his friends in the Norfolk Orthodox community the opportunity to invest. Hundreds did so.

Showing positive returns to early WexTrust investors, Shereshevsky recruited some of them, all with strong ties to the Orthodox community, to join the sales staff at the newly formed broker-dealer WexTrust Securities. Eight satisfied investors agreed to join the sales team and began earning commissions on sales to their families and friends. To help drum up business, Shereshevsky advertised the opportunities on a local radio station and took out ads in the community newspaper *Jewish Press*.

WexTrust was a fraud. The professional-looking offering documents described which specific property WexTrust would buy with the investor money raised in each offering. But Shereshevsky and Byers sometimes simply kept the money, using some for their personal expenses, some to pay commissions to the oblivious salespeople, and the rest to make Ponzi payments to earlier investors. In total, Wex-

Trust raised more than $255 million from 1,196 investors, the vast majority of them Orthodox Jews.

On August 11, 2009, the FBI knocked on Shereshevsky's door—and not a day too soon. He was scheduled to leave that day for London by way of Tel Aviv. He did not have a reservation for a return flight. Byers and Shereshevsky plead guilty in October 2010 and February 2011, Byers was sentenced to 156 months in prison, and Shereshevsky, as of this writing, is awaiting sentencing.

By the time he joined WexTrust, Shereshevsky had admitted to a few friends that he had "made mistakes" earlier in life and had come to Virginia for a fresh start. He resumed using his real name. He did not, however, share the fact of his past mistakes with the vast majority of WexTrust investors. He did not disclose that information in the company's offering documents, although prospective investors certainly would have thought it important to know that WexTrust's COO had been convicted of fraud. Nor did he tell his salespeople to make those disclosures to prospective investors.

The vigilant investor will learn two important things from Shereshevsky's story. First, fraudsters often leave town once their criminal records and unpaid civil judgments have tainted the pool of prospective marks. Like Shereshevsky, they seek a fresh start in a new place and often change their names. This can make things challenging as you begin your due diligence investigation. When Shereshevsky was arrested by the FBI, a search of courthouse records in Virginia would have yielded nothing suspicious about him. Investors who bothered to learn where else he had lived would have been able to do a search of records in New York and would have learned of his two previous convictions. Database services like LexisNexis offer a search similar to a courthouse records search that identifies all names associated with a single social security number. Searching under Shereshevsky's alias

(Heller) would pull up both of his names. If you do not have access to LexisNexis or a similar service, find an investigator who does. We use LexisNexis at Investor's Watchdog, and many attorneys subscribe to similar services for purposes of legal research.

The second thing to notice about Shereshevsky's case is that even his admission to past transgressions did not keep his Orthodox friends who knew about his prior "trouble" from investing with him. His friends probably took it as a mark of good character that he was willing to come clean. Most of us are suckers for stories of redemption, and all of us can think of stupid things that we did when we were younger but would never repeat now. Fraud is different. Investments are to a convicted fraudster what a beer is to an alcoholic. A "former" fraudster who dares go close to someone else's money is on a predictable and well-worn path to disaster. You do not want to invest with someone on that path.

The proliferation of cons targeting people of faith has led me to a firm rule in evaluating investments for my Investor's Watchdog clients: "If religion is close, stay away."

The Humanitarian

On March 30, 2009, John Min was on his way home to Seattle from a luxury ski vacation in Whistler, British Columbia. When he stopped his Mercedes S550 at the Blaine, Washington, border crossing, customs agents arrested him. He pleaded guilty in December 2009 to one count of wire fraud in connection with an affinity fraud that adds a twist to those that we've discussed so far.

Min convinced his investors, mostly members of Christian churches and the elderly, that his investments not only would pay them an attractive return, but would also serve the world's poor and needy. Through his companies, DIME Financial Group LLC and DIME Capital LLC, which he operated collectively under the name DIME FX, Min promised safe, low-risk investments that were suitable for retirees. He persuaded investors that he could generate those returns through trading foreign currencies, and that his track record of generating those returns was stellar. He claimed a bachelor's degree from Columbia University, which he had actually attended for only three semesters before leaving with a cumulative grade point average of 1.808. He told investors (falsely) that his trading was overseen by an advisory board that included an SEC attorney. There was no such board, and the SEC attorney had never heard of Min until he drew the interest of the SEC's enforcement staff.

To further the fraud, Min formed a separate company, DIME Foundation, as a nonprofit corporation and told investors that it would raise funds for charitable projects worldwide and would donate 100 percent of the funds raised to those projects. Min told prospective donors to DIME Foundation that the foundation gave microloans to the poor in the third world and supported charities benefiting widows and orphans in Bolivia. He staged meetings to raise funds for the DIME Foundation at which he also pitched investments in DIME FX. Min's charitable façade drew investors to a scheme that ultimately raised more than $6.4 million from 60 investors before the SEC shut it down. Min is now prisoner number 39242-086 at the Federal Correction Facility at Sheridan, Oregon, 90 miles south of Portland. He will leave prison in 2013.

Scamsters of all stripes, but especially affinity fraudsters targeting religious groups, often tout a charitable component. It lends credibility to the scam. *After all*, you are tempted to think, *if they can afford to give money away, they must be making plenty of it. And if my investments can help, so much the better.* The vigilant investor is wary of any supposedly profitable investment that attempts to tug at your heartstrings. It's a device intended to short-circuit your due diligence investigation.

The Radio Host

The Iranian American community in Los Angeles listened to John Farahi. From the Studio City offices of KIRN Radio—the only 24-hour Persian-language radio station in metropolitan Los Angeles—Farahi was the host of *The Economy Today*, an hourlong program that took calls from listeners and discussed economic developments. Many of his listeners were middle-aged to older immigrants who had fled Iran as adults in 1979 when the shah of Iran was overthrown. They came to America speaking only Persian and appreciated Farahi for bringing them news in their native tongue; they considered him an authority. Although he did not pitch investments on the radio program, over his eight years of hosting it, Farahi encouraged listeners to make an appointment at his investment advisory business, New Point Financial Services, Inc., if they needed help with investment decisions.

When the economy tanked in 2008 and the U.S. government created the Troubled Asset Relief Program (TARP), Farahi saw not disaster, but opportunity. According to the SEC, he told his exclusively Iranian American clientele that he could invest their savings in low-risk corporate bonds backed by the TARP fund. That pitch brought him more than $18 million. However, there were no such bonds. Instead, perhaps hoping to make good on his promise of steady returns, he used some of the money to make large, risky bets on stock options. As in the case of a roulette player who bets on black only to see the ball land on red, the money that Farahi bet on stock options disappeared instantly. He used the rest of it to make Ponzi payments and maintain himself and his family in style until the money ran out and the SEC came knocking.

Affinity fraudsters are especially successful with groups whose first language is not English. You can understand why. Many immigrants from non-English-speaking countries feel intimidated by the prospect of dealing with American advisers who speak only English. Those investors are fish in a barrel to an affinity fraudster who speaks not only their native language, but also the language of finance.

Farahi's status as a radio talk show host no doubt brought him many more marks than he would have met otherwise. In the past three years, Investor's Watchblog has covered four separate scams involving hosts of syndicated talk radio programs. It's important to understand that the purpose of most financial talk radio programs is marketing for the host's investment advisory business. He may be a terrific radio host, but being able to talk on cue is not a reliable indicator of trustworthiness. In fact, if you listen closely to the rapid-fire disclaimers at the beginning and/or ending of the show, you will usually learn that neither the radio station nor its advertisers endorse the host or his business.

Of course, most radio hosts are honest people who will tell you that you should not infer investing skill from their presence on the radio. What you *can* infer from their radio gig or from their involvement in any other outside business is that they have less time to pay attention to the investing side of their business. Unless they retain independent help in evaluating alternative investments, their opportunity to spot a scam before they recommend it to you is diminished.

Scam artists stick with what works, and affinity fraud works like nothing else. All good salespeople seek to bond with prospective customers over things that they have in common. There's nothing nefarious about that. But doing so with the intent to exploit those commonalities for criminal purposes sets affinity fraudsters apart from legitimate salespeople. Neither the SEC nor any other regulator can slow the torrid pace of affinity fraud. But as a vigilant investor, you can. Be on the lookout.

Due Diligence for the Vigilant

The vigilant investor:

▶ Looks at what she has in common with the investment promoter and his investors and is wary if there is too much in common

▶ Calculates what a promoter who guarantees an investment would have to pay if it were to collapse and considers whether the promoter has the cash to make that payment

▶ Understands that the FDIC covers only losses from bank closures and pays only depositors

▶ Reviews the insurance policy or CDS that is supposedly insuring against losses and confirms that coverage by calling the alleged insurer directly

▶ Does not let an investment promoter's devout persona or reputation deter her from a thorough background investigation

▶ Avoids any investment pitched by an appeal to religious faith

▶ Uses services like LexisNexis to search for the possibility that an investment promoter is operating under an assumed name

▶ Considers ties between a profit-making venture and philanthropy a reason to be cautious

▶ Understands that investment advisers' outside business ventures can distract them from paying attention to their investment advisory business

6

Only Amateurs Make It Sound Too Good to Be True

Tricks of the Trade and the Future of Financial Fraud

The most outrageous lies that can be invented will find
believers if a man only tells them with all his might.

—MARK TWAIN

In 1996, NBC's *Dateline* found a community in South Carolina where people earn their living as con artists. Every spring, some of the Irish Travellers in Murphy Village decamp and spread out across the country, running cons long and short: roofing scams, stolen property scams, home security scams—even investment scams.

There is something intriguing about an entire community of fraudsters. Perhaps when their children ask for a bedtime story, rather than "Little Red Riding Hood" or "The Three Little Pigs," or a sports story like Babe Ruth's legendary called home run, these kids go to sleep to stories about the legendary 25-year Ponzi scheme. "He was the Babe Ruth of what we do," the father might say. "After Madoff, the game was never the same."

Bernard Madoff did indeed change the game. Unless the SEC and state securities regulators keep pace, Ponzi schemes will forever be harder to spot, will last longer, and will rob more people of their life savings than they did before December 2008, when Madoff turned himself in. In this chapter, we will examine the chief lesson that Madoff taught the next generation of scam artists, look at several other scams and the tricks and tactics that made them successful, and learn how you can unmask the scamster who tries those tricks and tactics on you.

Promise Less for Success

The old axiom "If it sounds too good to be true, it probably is" is dangerous. It leads investors to believe that the chief identifying characteristic of an investment scam is a promise of outlandish returns. That is not the case, and the axiom therefore paves the way for fraudsters who are smart enough not to promise the moon. An accurate redrafting of the axiom would read, "If it sounds too good to be true, you are talking to an amateur scam artist."

Madoff understood that promising less would extend the life of his scam. Although the returns he claimed to deliver (10 to 17 percent) were suspicious in light of his seeming ability to produce those returns even in bad years for the stock market, they were not the 50 to 100 percent returns that the stereotypical scamster promises.

David Hernandez should have known better. From October 1998 to August 2001, he served a 34-month sentence in federal prison on charges of theft and wire fraud for using his position as a vice president at Chicago's Columbia National Bank to help himself to $590,000 in depositors' money. But in February 2008, not chastened by his prison stretch, Hernandez began operating a Ponzi scheme promising investors returns of 10 to 16 percent *per month* with no risk. Hernandez sold his marks "guaranteed investment contracts" by touting his business and banking experience and his law degree. He had neither the experience nor the degree. He promised investors that the investment contracts were insured products and therefore completely safe. There was no insurance, just a Ponzi scheme. Hernandez raised $11 million in 13 months before the SEC shut him down. In January 2010, he pleaded guilty to one count of mail fraud. He is now inmate number 22735-047 in the United States Penitentiary in Marion, Illinois, serving a 200-month sentence.

When I find a scam artist who promises a return of 100 percent per year, as Hernandez did, I know I am dealing with either a rookie scam artist or someone who has given absolutely no thought to the longevity of his scam. Remember, there is no profit-generating engine to create the promised return. To return 100 percent to Investor A, Hernandez would have had to use all of the money he conned from Investor B. When someone is promising that kind of return, the pressure to find new marks is unrelenting.

The lesson is that, while investments that sound too good to be true *are* too good to be true (the word *probably* in the classic axiom has cost investors billions), investments that sound reasonable might also be frauds. Every scam artist who has been paying attention is now offering returns that are only a percentage point or two above what investors can earn from legitimate, safe investments. As Madoff might say should he write a book on Ponzi schemes for dummies, anything more is a waste and puts unnecessary pressure on the scheme.

Remember what we learned in Chapter 1 about that sneaky congruence bias and how to combat it. The vigilant investor approaches every due diligence investigation—whether the investment promises 50 percent per year or 5 percent—with the determination not to confirm what she has been told, but to look for hints of fraud.

Being Anyone You Want to Be

Marc Dreier had impressive credentials. After earning an undergraduate degree from Yale and a law degree from Harvard, Dreier worked at some of New York's most prestigious law firms before opening his own firm, Dreier, LLP, in 1996. Dreier employed 250 attorneys and had a biweekly payroll of more than $2.5 million. Works by Picasso and Warhol lined the walls of his Park Avenue law offices. Dreier attracted the best and the brightest and appeared to be able to afford to pay the lavish salaries that he doled out to attract top legal talent.

In 2002, the pressure of maintaining both his law firm and his lifestyle led Dreier into the investment business. He began selling promissory notes, some of them issued by New York realty company Solow Realty. The only problem was that Solow Realty knew nothing about it.

With his Ivy League education and his apparent success, Dreier had no trouble attracting investors. In fact, 13 hedge funds bought almost $400 million in promissory notes (paying purported interest rates of between 7 and 12 percent), and individual investors snapped up what the hedge funds did not buy.

Dreier was running a con that would ultimately raise more than

$700 million, lead to his arrest on July 13, 2009, and land him in prison until 2026. If you have never heard of him, it is only because Bernard Madoff still dominated the headlines with his record-breaking scam. Dreier is now inmate number 70595-054 at the Sandstone Correctional Facility, 100 miles northeast of Minneapolis, Minnesota. He will be 86 years old when he walks out of prison, if he lives that long. But his legacy will live far beyond that day. Dreier's con taught scamsters two of the most audacious tricks that I have seen in more than 20 years of interviewing con men and wading through the wreckage of their schemes.

In November 2008, Dreier was soliciting a sale of a $33 million promissory note to a New York hedge fund. Dreier told the mark, the manager of the hedge fund, that an Icelandic hedge fund would issue the note and a large pension fund out of Ontario, Canada, would guarantee it. Dreier had communicated with the mark only over the telephone. Expecting the mark to make at least some attempt at a due diligence investigation, Dreier arranged for him to speak to the supposed guarantor of the note as well as to an official of the hedge fund based in Iceland. But how could he arrange a conversation between the mark and two people who did not exist except in Dreier's imagination? Enter former SEC enforcement attorney Robert Miller.

Robert Miller served on the enforcement staff of the SEC from 2000 to 2005. In exchange for $100,000, Miller agreed to pose as a representative of the Icelandic hedge fund and as a representative of the Ontario Teachers' Pension Plan, which supposedly guaranteed the note. Dreier provided Miller with cell phones that matched the dialing codes for Reykjavik and Toronto and an outline detailing what he should say in response to specific questions. The mark made the calls, and Miller fulfilled his end of the bargain. Dreier wired him $100,000.

But Miller's telephonic theatrical debut was underwhelming. The mark was still unconvinced. So Dreier hatched a scheme to arrange a face-to-face meeting with the mark at the offices of the $100 billion Ontario Teachers' Pension Plan. On the pretense of seeking legal work from the organization, Dreier scheduled a meeting with its general counsel one hour before his scheduled meeting with the mark. As is customary, the two men exchanged business cards. When the meeting was over, Dreier remained in the conference room. When the mark arrived, Dreier met him in the lobby, introduced himself as the general counsel for the Ontario Teachers' Pension Plan, and handed the mark the general counsel's business card.

The trick was bold, and it might have worked had the mark not been so diligent. The hedge fund manager who met with Dreier that day deserves a spot in the Due Diligence Hall of Fame. Before leaving, the hedge fund manager asked the receptionist, "Is that the general counsel?"

"No," she said, and called the police. Dreier, who was lingering in the conference room to maintain the illusion that he worked for the organization, was arrested by the Toronto police and charged with impersonation. When he was released on bail and returned to New York five days later, FBI agents were waiting for him. His six-year charade was over.

As it turns out, the scheme would have collapsed even if the hedge fund manager had not been so diligent. One of Dreier's hedge fund clients had called Solow Realty to inquire about an overdue interest payment, and Solow learned for the first time that Dreier had commandeered the firm to enrich himself.

Seemingly obvious questions unmasked a sophisticated scam. And yet 13 hedge fund managers failed to ask the right questions before giving Dreier $400 million. You might think that it would take a team of forensic accountants to uncover a scam as large and well disguised as Dreier's, but it doesn't. A few probes can determine whether a seemingly successful investment business is a castle on a strong foundation or a house of cards.

Ask stupid questions. Talk to the people from whom the profits supposedly flow. In Dreier's case, it was Solow Realty. A single phone call to confirm that Solow had issued the promissory notes would have unmasked the scam in its first week. As to how to unmask one person impersonating another, use the Internet. Look for the Facebook page, the LinkedIn page, or the Twitter account for the person you supposedly just met. You might find a photograph there. If not, LexisNexis, in addition to the courthouse records information it can give you, will give you a date of birth. Does that information match the person you just met, or was the person you met 20 years older than the person she claimed to be?

Why didn't anyone else ask the "stupid" questions earlier in the Dreier case? Dreier gave the answer in a *60 Minutes* interview: "It was clear to me that the more you showed people that you didn't need money, the easier it was to attract money. So having the trappings of success was a very important part of the plan."

Dreier is right: It's easier to attract money if you look as if you don't need it. But asking questions aimed at unmasking someone who appears to have earned vast success seems like the height of effrontery; the kind of insult that would have sent eighteenth-century gentlemen to their dueling pistols. The vigilant investor resolves that dilemma in one of three ways: (1) by asking those questions, politeness be damned; (2) by hiring someone to ask those questions; or (3) by saying no to the investment. Following any other course is dangerous.

Tracking the Headlines

When Al Gore landed in Stockholm to accept the 2007 Nobel Peace Prize, little did he know that his crusade for an environmental awakening had helped to launch several financial scams. *An Inconvenient Truth*, the documentary of his presentation about global warming, had opened in May 2006 at the Sundance Film Festival and won two Academy Awards in January 2007. In September 2006 (four months after *An Inconvenient Truth* debuted), Aerokinetic Energy Corporation of Sarasota, Florida, put out a press release announcing the creation of its new energy technology called "Leonardo." According to Aerokinetic, Leonardo was "capable of creating fuel-less electrical energy at a fraction of the cost of conventional or nuclear means, without generating any pollution." Leonardo, the press release said, was not wind dependent because it harvested energy from nonmoving (still) air and thus could be placed inside a building, making it the first indoor wind turbine. Its power output was 95 percent efficient, and it could run 24/7 without pollution.

The company announced that it had already developed and built a power station that proved the technology and provided a consistent source of power. It supposedly held patents for all of its founder's inventions, including Leonardo and an electric car dubbed "Raphael." According to Aerokinetic, many companies and municipalities had recognized Leonardo's potential and signed contracts to begin using Leonardo to generate power. The only challenge the company faced was keeping up with the flood of orders.

Although Aerokinetic was a real company, Leonardo consisted of nothing more than a child's swing set ordered off eBay modified with magnets. Beyond that, all of Aerokinetic's claims were only untested assertions of what Aerokinetic "would like to build" in the future.

Aerokinetic's founder did not hold a patent on Leonardo or Raphael (or any of the other Teenage Mutant Ninja Turtles). Before the SEC could shut down Aerokinetic in July 2008, the company had used its false claims, bolstered by the public consciousness raised by Gore's prize, to raise more than $500,000 by selling stock in the company.

As the Aerokinetic case illustrates, scam artists track the headlines more closely than even the most energetic news junkie, because headlines give them the credibility that they so desperately need if they are to make a sale. Whether it is the price of gold, the need for technology to cap deep-sea oil wells, or developments in the search for a cure for cancer, scam artists will always use the headlines to launch new scams.

The vigilant investor—remembering what he has learned about press releases—insists on a thorough investigation of any opportunity that seems especially timely. Claims of patents can be investigated at the U.S. Patent and Trademark Office at http://www.uspto.gov. All you have to do is call the supposed end users of the revolutionary new product or service and ask how much of it the end user has bought. Insist on time to do your investigation, and say no to anyone who pushes for an immediate decision.

The Celebrity Factor

Raffaello Follieri came to America in his early twenties and presented himself as a representative of the Vatican, sent to the United States to help the Catholic Church sell church properties to meet the costs of the church's financial settlements in child abuse cases. Before he left Italy, Follieri had befriended the nephew of Cardinal Angelo Sadano, who was Vatican secretary of state under Pope John Paul II. Claiming other substantial relationships at the Vatican as well, Follieri raised hundreds of thousands of dollars from wealthy New Yorkers, telling them that he would use his connections to buy church properties at a discount; develop them into schools, office space, or housing; and then sell them at a substantial profit.

Claiming that he had graduated from the University of Rome, which he had attended only briefly, with degrees in law and economics, Follieri convinced dozens of wealthy investors that his business plan was promising. Determined to portray a successful image, Follieri used money from his initial investors to buy designer clothes and rent an apartment in Trump Tower. While he did bid on church properties, he was never the high bidder and initially failed to buy even a single property.

Follieri met Anne Hathaway, star of *The Princess Diaries*, *Rachel Getting Married*, and *The Devil Wears Prada*, through a mutual friend, and the two dated for four years. Follieri walked innumerable red carpets with Hathaway, met her thespian colleagues, and had his picture in every celebrity magazine. Hathaway served on the board of the Follieri Foundation, whose mission was to inoculate children in third-world countries.

Follieri leveraged his celebrity and supposed connections with the Vatican into a brief meeting with former President Clinton and a friendship of sorts with Doug Band, a Clinton aide and gatekeeper. Band, in turn, introduced Follieri to very wealthy people, some of whom were willing to back his enterprise.

Through the Clinton connection, Follieri met supermarket magnate Ron Burkle. Burkle formed a venture with Follieri to buy and develop church properties, agreeing to commit up to $105 million to a joint venture with Follieri named Follieri Yucaipa Investments, Inc. (Follieri Yucaipa). Follieri convinced Burkle that he needed an operating budget to travel and identify potentially profitable properties. He used that budget to whisk Hathaway around the globe in private jets, ensconce the two of them in five-star hotels, rent a $36,000-per-month high-rise apartment overlooking St. Patrick's Cathedral, and fund one round of inoculations through the Follieri Foundation.

Follieri also used the operating budget from Burkle to set up offices on Park Avenue. He hired nuns to work at the reception desk and built an altar in the office to better maintain his image as a humble Catholic. With funding from Burkle, Follieri was able to buy a few church properties, none of which proved profitable.

Spending money faster than he could raise it and facing demands from Burkle for documentation showing that his operating expenses were legitimate, Follieri pressed his employees to create phony invoices to send to Burkle. Eventually, Burkle sued Follieri for misappropriating more than $1 million of the Follieri Yucaipa operating budget. But, no doubt lured by the same image that had ensnared Follieri's earlier investors, hedge fund Plainfield Asset Management, Inc., based in Greenwich, Connecticut, agreed to pay to settle the Burkle lawsuit and give Follieri additional funding.

When the Department of Justice finally caught up with Follieri in June 2008, he was planning a blowout birthday bash for himself on the Isle of Capri and preparing to replicate his long con in Europe and elsewhere. In November 2008, the U.S. District Court for the Southern District of New York sentenced him to 54 months in prison on charges of money laundering and wire fraud. Hathaway dumped him. He is now inmate number 61143-054 at the Federal Correction Institution at Loretto in southwestern Pennsylvania. He gets out in May 2012. He will be only 33. Watch out for him.

Scamsters with less flare than Follieri also play on our national obsession with celebrity. In my first assignment as a court-appointed receiver in an SEC fraud case, I interviewed several victims of a scam called Success Trust and Holdings, LLC, which supposedly generated large returns by leveraging the value of investors' real estate. When I asked investors what had led them to place their trust in the company's founder, "Dr." Archie Paul Reynolds, many of them cited seeing the photograph of Dr. Reynolds receiving an award from President George W. Bush. A few even said that it was the picture that overcame all of their doubts about the investment. I have seen the picture. Mr. and Mrs. Reynolds are there with a smiling George and Laura Bush. There is no award in the shot—no plaque, no medal, no certificate. Just the kind of photo that you can get by making the maximum contribution to the president's reelection campaign.

Follieri had his own version of the photo with the president. By pledging $50 million from the Follieri Foundation to the Clinton Global Initiative, Follieri earned a public acknowledgment of his generosity from President Clinton. He also took Hathaway to meet Pope John Paul II, failing to mention that the "audience" and the blessing they received was something that His Holiness granted to any believer who came to the Vatican on a certain day of the month.

Scam artists understand the power of celebrity and will cultivate every opportunity to draw close to someone famous, even for a moment. The vigilant investor avoids long con artists like Follieri by viewing supposed connections with celebrity and power not as indicators of credibility, but as potential efforts to overwhelm the investor and short-circuit a careful consideration of the proposed investment. Connections to celebrity and power are so often tools of the long con artist that they should be discounted altogether.

In meetings with a prospective investment partner, give no indication that you are aware of any supposed connections to celebrity and power; interview the investment promoter as if you know nothing about him. The long con artist cannot resist skillfully injecting refer-

ences to powerful or famous people. A legitimate investment promoter respects any legitimate relationships with celebrities or
politicians—especially if they are investors—enough not to use them
in his sales efforts. Consider how comfortable you would be with the
investment promoter using *your* name to solicit new investors. Beware
of the name-dropper.

Renting Credibility

Ulysses S. Grant owed his success in the Civil War at least partially to
his ability to judge which of the officers under his command had the
talent, nerve, courage, and dependability to get the job done. Sher-
man, Thomas, Sheridan—he rarely chose poorly. After Appomattox,
Grant served as secretary of war in President Andrew Johnson's cabi-
net. He rode his popularity to victory in the 1868 and 1872 presiden-
tial elections, retaining the love and devotion of those who had served
with him, despite a bribery scandal that tarnished his reputation,
although it never implicated him directly.

At the close of his time in the White House, Grant needed a
vacation. Hoping that a warm reception overseas—and reports of it
back home—would help Americans remember him as a hero of the
Civil War, Grant, his wife, Julia, and their youngest son, Jesse,
embarked on a two-year journey around the globe. When they
returned home, they were short on money and short of their goal of
restoring Grant's reputation enough to secure him another Republican
nomination for president. The family settled down in New York, and
Grant, who had never had much luck outside the military, searched
for a way to support his family.

Grant's son Buck convinced him that the securities industry was the answer. Buck introduced Grant to Ferdinand Ward, who had been so successful as a stock trader in the years immediately after the Civil War that he proudly carried the title "Young Napoleon of Wall Street." Ward had an enormous estate in Connecticut and a lavish town house in New York. He was handsome. He was articulate. Think of a cross between Brad Pitt and Bill Clinton.

Grant went into business with his son and Ward, forming the firm of Grant & Ward. Grant persuaded many of his old Army comrades to invest with the firm. They sent him their pensions, and things seemed to go well at first. But unbeknownst to Grant, Ward was the Bernard Madoff of the nineteenth century. Ward never invested any of the money that flowed into the firm. Instead, he spent the money to maintain himself in opulent comfort. He used the constant flow of cash to make dividend payments to early investors, including the veterans who had preserved the Union. As all such schemes do, Ward's collapsed when he could no longer raise enough money from new investors to keep up with withdrawals by existing clients.

Having sold everything he owned in an attempt to pay back those who had trusted him, Grant was once again penniless. Only the successful publication of his memoirs (with the help of his friend Mark Twain), finished just three days before his death from throat cancer, spared Julia Grant penury in her widowhood.

Most of the brave men who had fought under Grant, some of whom had left arms or legs at Shiloh, Petersburg, or Lookout Mountain, knew that Grant had led them through a life-and-death struggle to preserve the Union. He had been a good steward of a two-million-man Army and leader of the nation that he had helped save. How could he fail to be a good steward of their meager $10 per month? When he said that he could help them protect and grow their pensions, they believed him. But the veterans who lost their pensions to

Grant & Ward had never met Ferdinand Ward, much less considered that there might be something ugly behind his handsome and successful façade. It was good enough for them that General Grant trusted him.

More than a century later, savvy scam artists still use the tactic that proved so lucrative for Ferdinand Ward. Rather than do the long, tedious work of building a trusting relationship with each of her intended marks personally, the smart scamster instead finds people who have already gained the trust of many people and recruits them as unwitting accomplices to the scam. People follow their trusted advisers into a scam just as Grant's Civil War comrades followed him into battle and into financial ruin.

Bernie Madoff used this tactic. The vast majority of his investors came to him through "feeder funds," other hedge funds managed by other investment advisers, each of whom had the trust of his clients. Investors in those feeder funds had never met Bernie Madoff, but they knew their own adviser and trusted him implicitly. If Madoff had wooed each of his victims personally, his scam would have been much smaller, and the chances are good that at least one of those individual investors would have asked questions that would have led to Madoff's undoing sooner.

Investment fraudsters sometimes pay a high price to rent the credibility of others in the form of commissions payable to the investment adviser or insurance agent or accountant who convinces her trusting clients to invest with the fraudster. Of course, that commission blinds the otherwise trustworthy adviser to the truth about the scam into which she is leading her trusting clients. Seeing the flow of money short-circuits a disciplined due diligence process. The vigilant investor asks his trusted adviser what commission he is earning on the sale. If the adviser is earning any commission, then you should either avoid the investment altogether or do your own due diligence.

The Test-Drive

David Copperfield has walked through the Great Wall of China and made the Statue of Liberty disappear, and Chris Angel has taken Harry Houdini's water torture trick up a notch, locking himself upside down in a water-filled glass coffin suspended several stories above the ground. Two minutes after Angel enters the water-filled coffin, it crashes to the pavement. If he doesn't perform the trick successfully, Angel will either drown or hit the asphalt like a bug on a windshield.

Copperfield and Angel would agree that they are masters of illusion, not magic. But to those who do not know the trick, their acts might as well be magic. We are at such a loss to explain what we have seen that magic almost becomes an acceptable explanation. Anyone who encounters an investment scamster is likely to encounter an equally powerful illusion.

The scam artist's grand finale is called the *test-drive*. It is the illusion that leads most investors in a Ponzi scheme to truly believe that they have invested in a legitimate profit-making venture. They believe it like they believe that the sun will rise tomorrow or that Barry Bonds knowingly took steroids. And, yet, as with any other "magic trick," there is an ordinary explanation for the test-drive illusion that seems obvious once you know it.

We start with the common assumptions of the audience (investors, in this case). No one trusts anyone else more than she trusts herself. In the matters that are most important to them, people insist on seeing things for themselves, on being able to say that they saw something or heard something personally. We start, therefore, with the realization that people tend to believe what they see and hear for themselves.

"You mean I can earn 2 percent per month, guaranteed?" you say. "I don't believe it."

"It's true," your adviser says. "I have 10 customers who are earning that return right now."

"How can that possibly be?" you ask.

"The trader who runs the program has access to medium-term notes that he trades on a platform that is usually reserved for the top 10 financial institutions in the world. He gets the notes at a discount and already has buyers lined up at face value."

"That doesn't make economic sense," you say. "I've been to college, taken finance and economics, and that is simply not possible."

"It's okay if you want to pass, but I might be able to find a way for you to see for yourself."

"That's the only possible way I'd ever believe this," you respond.

"Well," says your adviser, "there are plenty of people clamoring to get into this thing, but you and I have known each other a long time, and I don't want you to lose this opportunity. So, I'll tell you what. The minimum investment is $250,000. If I can find someone who's willing to put in just $240,000, I could ask the trader if he'd let you in for $10,000. I could pool your $10,000 with the $240,000 and meet the minimum investment that way between the two of you. Would that interest you if I can make it happen?"

Despite your skepticism, you have already started calculating how much you could make on an investment that pays 2 percent per month, even if it works for only a few months. So you say, "Okay."

"I don't know if I can pull it off, but I'll let you know if we get lucky," your adviser tells you.

A few days go by, and your broker calls to say that he has worked it out. You give him a check for $10,000 and count the days on the calendar. In 30 days, you receive a check for $200. You receive another check 30 days later, and yet another 30 days after that. And you are hooked. You've seen it with your own eyes—you've taken a test-drive and liked the feel of the thing. You kick yourself for not putting in the $250,000 initially. You calculate the money that you lost by being cautious, and you ask your adviser whether you can jump in for the full $250,000.

"I'll see if we're still accepting subscriptions," he says. "There is a maximum that we can raise, and I have to check to see whether we've reached it." You pray that you are not too late.

Finally the word comes back that the investment is almost fully subscribed, but that you can just get in under the wire. You invest the IRA rollover money from your old job. You write the check for $250,000 and think about how lucky you are.

You'll probably get a check for $5,000 the first month. You may even blow it on an extravagance, since you're sure that those checks will keep coming. You've seen it for yourself, after all.

After spending a couple more $5,000 checks, you start to wonder why you aren't letting it ride by reinvesting the profits. So, rather than getting a check each month, you look forward to receiving your monthly statement. Month after month, it shows your account balance rising so quickly that you begin to peruse the Luxury Estates section of Friday's *Wall Street Journal*.

When the SEC shuts down the scam, you are only marginally irritated at the inconvenience, believing that in a few days or weeks, the SEC will see for itself that the investment is legitimate and allow it to continue as before. You've seen it work with your own eyes, and not even the SEC's interest can convince you that anything is amiss.

But the SEC has seen this trick before, too, and it knows what is going on behind the curtain. The money you have been receiving every month is your principal. You have been withdrawing your own money, just as if you had been taking it out of a savings account. Only, in this case, several strangers have also been making withdrawals.

There never were any profits. If you invested $250,000, the scam artist will be more than happy to send you back $100,000 in monthly distribution payments. He is still ahead by $150,000.

The vigilant investor never gets behind the wheel of any investment until she has kicked the tires. The test-drive illusion is powerful and hard to resist. Make it a hard-and-fast rule: "Not a single dollar goes in until I have done my due diligence."

The Takeaway Pitch

The savvy scamster knows that you worry about being ripped off, so he'll invoke Bernie Madoff's name and assume the role of your protector. "You can't be too careful," the scamster will say. "I've been in this business a long time, and I've seen plenty of Bernie Madoffs. You have to do your homework." Of course, the scamster uses this tactic to insinuate himself into your circle of trusted advisers. *Why would he warn me about a scam if he were running one?* Reject the invitation.

Close on the heels of warning you to be on your guard against scamsters will come a reminder that the current opportunity is open for only a limited time: "The window closes on Friday." If you continue to ask questions, the salesperson may even seem to lose interest in you, saying that he needs to attend to the needs of those who are ready to jump in. The parting will be cordial. The scamster knows that the seed that he has planted will germinate in your mind. When you call to ask one final question, the salesperson may not even take your call right away. He knows that if you are still thinking about the investment, he can afford to pull out what we call the *takeaway* pitch. When you finally connect, the scamster will probably tell you that the investment is fully subscribed and that he cannot accept any more investments. "Will there be another opportunity anytime soon?" you'll ask.

"It's hard to say. These things come around now and again, but I can't say when there will be another chance. You have to be prepared to jump in quickly when the window opens."

The scamster's takeaway pitch (taking away your opportunity) uses another cognitive bias that occurs in all healthy humans: the loss aversion bias. First identified by Daniel Kahneman and Amos Tversky in 1979, the loss aversion bias says that humans value avoiding losses twice as much as they do acquiring gains. When the scamster makes you feel as if you have lost a fantastic opportunity, he knows that you will be doubly motivated to avoid that loss if at all possible. When he calls you the next day to say that an investor dropped out at the last minute and that there is room for one more, your loss aversion bias will throw you into a life-altering financial collision . . . unless you are a vigilant investor.

The vigilant investor recognizes the takeaway pitch for what it is: an attempt to refocus her attention in a way that will short-circuit a thorough due diligence investigation. If someone takes away an opportunity for incredible guaranteed returns, send a thank-you note and leave it at that.

Working the Edges of the Law

Scam artists frequently cite federal securities law in the offering documents that describe their scheme. They do so not to comply with it, but to give you the impression that they have fully researched the law and determined that their investment complies with it. You will see citations to Regulation D, which allows for the sale of unregistered securities to accredited investors. You will see references to Rules 504, 505, and 506, which govern the number of investors allowed and the amount of money that can be raised in certain unregistered offerings.

A favorite among scam artists is Section 3(a)(3) of the Securities Act of 1933. It exempts from registration "any note . . . which arises out of a current transaction or the proceeds of which have been or are to be used for current transactions, and which has a maturity at the time of issuance of not exceeding nine months." Scamsters love to sell promissory notes, citing Section 3(a)(3) for the proposition that notes that mature in nine months or less are exempt from registration. But the exemption applies only to high-grade commercial paper traded by major corporations, not to promissory notes sold in connection with an unregistered investment. Scamsters find Section 3(a)(3) especially useful because it appears to say what the scamsters want it to say. Unless you were trained in securities law, you would never know the truth.

Promissory note scams are an epidemic. If you find a promissory note investment claiming exemption under Section 3(a)(3), stay away. At the very least, you know that the promoter is ignorant of the law. At most, you know that he is stealing from investors. Call the SEC and your state securities commissioner.

Making the call to the SEC might actually be lucrative for you. One of the more intriguing provisions of the Dodd-Frank Act is the whistle-blower provision, which offers a bounty of at least 10 percent of disgorgement and civil penalties that the SEC collects above $1 million to the person who first discloses evidence of a scam. Reporting a scam that yields a $10 million payment of disgorgement and penalties would bring you $900,000. A trained force of vigilant investors can not only make the investing landscape safer, but receive rewards for doing so.

The Dead to Me Approach

An assignment for an Investor's Watchdog client took me to London and then to Geneva, Switzerland, where I met with representatives from several Swiss private banks (the kind that keep the fabled numbered accounts). A select few had not fallen victim to Bernard Madoff. I asked them how it was that they had been able to avoid Madoff when so many other Swiss private banks had led their clients into the biggest Ponzi scheme in history. One of the bankers could not have been more forthright. "We did not know it was a fraud," he said. "We had some questions and could not get the answers. So we did not invest."

Please notice the discipline implied in that statement. The bank could not get answers to its questions. Therefore, the bank did not invest. What happens all too often is, "I asked questions. I did not get the answers. But have you seen the returns that Bob is getting?! I've got to get into this before I miss out on any more profits."

The Swiss banker aptly described the approach to due diligence that any vigilant investor will take. I call it the *dead to me* approach. If you have questions and you do not get the answers, think of the investment as dead to you. Now, dead means dead. Not mostly dead. Not on life support. Not something that CPR could revive. Stone-cold dead. Put it out of your mind and get on to whatever is next. You may hear of the investment again when the SEC launches an emergency enforcement action to shut it down. When you do, please call us to report that the dead to me approach worked for you.

The Future

There is a section on the Investor's Watchdog web site called The Crystal Ball, where we warn about the scams of the future, like alternative energy scams, health-care scams, and certificate of deposit scams. If a new trend makes the news, there will be an investment scam tied to it not far behind. Whatever the subject matter at the heart of these scams may be, one thing is certain: Because of Madoff, they will forever be harder to spot. They will promise less, give the impression of compliance with the federal securities laws, and look legitimate in every way. Industry standard due diligence will find confirmation for all material facts. *It all checks out,* pension funds and individual investors alike will think, just before they set fire to their money. But the vigilant investor will find the truth, expose even well-disguised scams, and save not only his own nest egg but the nest eggs of every investor who would have come after.

Due Diligence for the Vigilant

The vigilant investor:

- ▶ Understands that the most dangerous scams look perfectly legitimate and never sound too good to be true
- ▶ Confirms the identity of those who vouch for an investment
- ▶ Talks to people at the business from which the money flows to confirm the salesperson's representations
- ▶ Remembers that scam artists love the headlines and is suspicious of any investment that seems especially timely
- ▶ Checks on claims of patents for new technology through the U.S. Patent and Trademark Office

➤ Confirms the use and profitability of new technology by talking to the end users

➤ Is never blinded by celebrity or power and avoids investments offered by name-droppers

➤ Remembers that savvy scamsters rent the credibility of those whom others trust and questions trusted advisers about commissions that they receive from any investment that they recommend

➤ Says no to a test-drive of an uncommonly profitable investment

➤ Never accepts a salesperson's offer to serve as the investor's protector and stays alert to the effects of the loss aversion bias

➤ Remembers that citing the law does not indicate compliance with the law

➤ Accepts her public duty to help expose investment crime

The Securities Industry

*Hunting the Wolf with the
Million-Dollar Smile*

7

Truth, Lies, and "Why Don't They Supervise?"

Inside Boiler Rooms and Other Brokerage Firms

With an evening coat and a white tie, anybody, even a stockbroker, can gain a reputation for being civilized.

—OSCAR WILDE

Fueled by cocaine, Quaaludes, and hookers, between 1990 and 1997, Jordan Belfort led a bacchanalian romp of a life as the CEO of broker-dealer (the industry term for a brokerage firm) Stratton Oakmont, Inc. The "Wolf of Wall Street," as Belfort was known, commuted to Stratton Oakmont's Long Island office by limousine and often went by helicopter to Manhattan to party. The least successful of his brokers made hundreds of thousands of dollars a year by bullying investors into buying the stocks of companies that Belfort controlled. Their idea of after-work fun was watching a pretty blonde assistant have her head shaved in exchange for money for breast augmentation surgery.

What Stratton Oakmont became is what all brokerage firms—even the biggest, most respected firms on Wall Street—can become in the absence of strong regulation and stiff enforcement: corrupt, abusive, and extremely profitable. This is the natural state of things. Firms succeed in resisting the pull toward becoming Stratton Oakmonts to varying degrees, but none of them is pure. Compliance bulwarks, which are supposed to detect and stop customer abuse, are as porous as the border between the United States and Mexico.

In this chapter, we begin our tour of the dark corners of the securities industry. Along the way, we will correct some common misconceptions about brokers and brokerage firms and look at brokers in various types of firms: boiler rooms, traditional firms, and independent firms. What we see on that tour will better equip the vigilant investor to protect his savings.

Naked Aggression: Inside the Boiler Room

Jordan Belfort ran Stratton Oakmont as a large pump-and-dump scheme. He controlled millions of shares of 34 different companies. Like Russian mobster Simeon Mogilevich, discussed in Chapter 4, Belfort told his brokers which stocks to push and when. He then sold his own stake once they had driven the prices up enough to guarantee him a multimillion-dollar profit.

Stratton Oakmont was a boiler room. Boiler rooms take their name from the intense pressure to sell. Like Stratton Oakmont, most boiler room firms consist of a large room filled with cubicles or desks, with a computer and a telephone on each desk. Dialing from lists of likely investors, licensed brokers cold-call prospects and use every device possible (some of which we'll discuss in Chapter 9) to convince the investor to buy what the broker is selling.

Like all brokers, before selling securities, Stratton Oakmont's brokers[1] had to pass a test called the Series 7 examination. Overall, 70 percent of the Series 7 exam tests the prospective broker's understanding of the rules and regulations that are designed to protect the broker's customers. But the Series 7 examination is in no way comparable in difficulty to the bar exam, medical boards, or CPA exams. Most prospective brokers pass it on their first attempt. As a tool for keeping bad brokers out of the industry, the Series 7 exam is about as effective as a driver's license test is at keeping bad drivers off the road. The CRD report from your state securities regulator will tell you whether your broker passed the Series 7 exam on the first attempt.

Brokerage firms are no better than the Series 7 exam at screening out brokers who are willing to abuse investors. While firms choose their new brokers carefully, they screen them primarily for their ability to attract new customers and sell securities, not for their integrity or deep knowledge of complex principles. If Warren Buffett couldn't sell stock to his grandmother, Belfort would have had no use for him as a broker.

The SEC and the U.S. Justice Department eventually caught up with Belfort. In May 1999, he pleaded guilty to money laundering and securities fraud. His sentencing was delayed as part of a deal in which he cooperated in the government's investigation of other pump-and-dump scamsters. He served 22 months in federal prison and was released in 2006. Ever the salesman, Belfort now travels the globe as a motivational speaker and conducts sales training seminars, sharing the sales method that he perfected at Stratton Oakmont.

Martin Scorsese is turning Jordan Belfort's memoir, *The Wolf of Wall Street*, into a motion picture starring Leonardo DiCaprio.

The vigilant investor recognizes a boiler room by the pitch. It almost always comes via a cold call. You'll never have heard of the broker or the firm she works for, but she wants you to buy stock right now. She'll tell you impressive lies about her firm and the stock she is selling. She won't take no for an answer. You'll have to hang up on her. Do that sooner rather than later. If the broker calls again, tell her that you are about to hang up again, and that you are calling the SEC as soon as you do so. Then call the nearest SEC regional office to report a boiler room. You can find a list of the SEC offices at www.sec.gov/contact/addresses.htm.

You Can't Keep a Bad Man Down

The story of Irving Stitsky, one of Belfort's cohorts at Stratton Oakmont, shows what becomes of brokers who are barred from the securities industry for abusing customers. Stitsky was a managing director at Stratton Oakmont. He supplied the pressure that motivated brokers to make money for Jordan Belfort. When the SEC closed Stratton Oakmont in 1997, he managed to avoid indictment and SEC charges.

Figuring that he was as good at escaping prosecution as he was at selling stocks, Stitsky immediately set out to use what he had learned at Stratton Oakmont. He and several cohorts acquired millions of shares of worthless stocks and promoted them on the Internet. When the "pump" had had the desired effect, they "dumped" the shares on innocent investors.

The FBI arrested Stitsky in August 1999 and charged him with money laundering, tax fraud, and conspiracy. In 2002, he pleaded guilty to one count of money laundering and was sentenced to 21 months in prison, followed by three years of supervised release. In September 2003, the SEC officially barred him from the securities industry.

In 2004, when he was released from prison, Stitsky used his "supervised release" to set up yet another fraudulent sales operation. He and two cohorts created an organization called Cobalt. Through a sales operation supervised by Stitsky, they told investors that Cobalt would profit by developing multifamily real estate properties. Stitsky and his cohorts raised more than $23 million from more than 250 investors and spent the money as if it were their own.

The FBI arrested Stitsky again in March 2006 and charged him with conspiracy and securities fraud. He fought the charges, but on November 23, 2009, a jury found him guilty on all five counts. At his sentencing hearing, U.S. District Judge Kimba Wood called him an "inveterate con man" and sentenced him to 85 years in prison. Stitsky is now inmate number 57309-053 in the Metropolitan Detention Center in Brooklyn. He is appealing his conviction.

The vigilant investor understands that brokers who have been kicked out of the industry rarely go back to school to become dental hygienists. Selling investments is what they know, and they keep right on selling them without a license. Use the search function on the SEC's web site to find out whether the SEC has shown a particular broker the door. Request a CRD from your state securities regulator to learn about other regulatory actions. The web site for the Federal Bureau of Prisons (www.bop.gov) can tell you whether a broker has served federal time. Don't be surprised if you find out that he has. Like Stitsky, boiler room brokers—whether they are registered or barred—are a persistent bunch. It's what makes them successful sales-people.

Bad Brokers, "Good" Firms, and Unauthorized Trading

William and Doris Pitera were elderly retirees from Fall River, Massachusetts. They had been married for 49 years and had one daughter. William had a high school education and worked as an electrician. Doris did not graduate from high school. But through decades of hard work, frugal living, and disciplined saving, the Piteras had accumulated a nest egg of $2.9 million.

Stephen Toussaint was a senior vice president and a very productive broker for the Boston branch office of the brokerage firm Oppenheimer & Co.[2] He had been the Piteras' broker for 12 years; they had followed him to Oppenheimer from a previous firm because they trusted him. In 2003, William, then 82, was diagnosed with Alzheimer's disease. He no longer recognized Doris or their daughter.

When Toussaint learned of William's Alzheimer's diagnosis, he began buying and selling stocks in the Piteras' accounts at a feverish pace, earning a commission on each trade. Over a 23-month period, Toussaint placed 1,616 trades in the Piteras' accounts (an average of more than three trades every weekday), all of them without the Piteras' permission. By doing so, Toussaint generated more than $800,000 in commissions for Oppenheimer.

What Toussaint did is called *churning*, the buying and selling of securities to generate commissions for the broker rather than for any sensible investment purpose. For reasons we'll identify later, it happens often.

But Toussaint was not satisfied with the huge commissions he earned through churning the Piteras' accounts. Beginning in July 2003, he forged 19 checks on one of their accounts, making them out to himself and depositing them in his personal bank account. The checks totaled $350,000.

Oppenheimer should have known that Toussaint was churning the Piteras' accounts. Commissions from trading in their accounts represented 85 percent of all of Toussaint's commissions in 2003, and 63 percent in 2004. Those figures are glaring enough to put even the most inexperienced manager on notice of possible misconduct by the broker.

However, Toussaint's branch manager had reason to protect him. The manager's compensation agreement paid him a bonus calculated as a percentage of the commissions that his brokers—including Toussaint—brought into the firm. According to Massachusetts Secretary of State William Galvin, who commenced an enforcement action against Oppenheimer, Toussaint continued to collect commissions from his outrageously excessive trading for a full year after Oppenheimer had reason to know that he had stolen $350,000 from his client.

In fact, according to Galvin, Oppenheimer actually covered up Toussaint's theft. When the head of security at Toussaint's bank contacted the firm about what he suspected were stolen funds deposited into Toussaint's bank account, Oppenheimer said, "Everything is fine."[3] The bank's head of security was so taken aback by Oppenheimer's response, and so concerned that Toussaint was stealing from the Piteras, that he called Bristol County Elder Services and explained the situation to them.

Attempting to conceal his conduct from investigators, Toussaint called Mrs. Pitera and admitted that he had written the forged checks. But he lied to her, claiming that the forged checks were reimbursement for securities that he had bought for her with his personal funds. He begged her to verify his story, saying that exposure would do serious damage to his children. Believing Toussaint's lies, Mrs. Pitera affirmed his bogus explanation.

Even when Oppenheimer decided, in February 2005, that it could no longer cover up for Toussaint, he was not fired. He was permitted to resign, leaving no mark on his record, and he moved on to take a job as a broker at Bank of America Investment Services, Inc. In 2008, he pleaded guilty to securities fraud charges stemming from his misconduct at Oppenheimer and was sentenced to 46 months in federal prison.

Brokerage firm branch managers are supposed to monitor their brokers for possible customer abuse. But branch managers sometimes remain deliberately, obtusely ignorant of customer abuse, for selfish reasons.

Oppenheimer is a traditional brokerage firm, like industry giants Smith Barney, UBS Financial Services, and Merrill Lynch. It operates with the same model of broker supervision, having a branch manager as the first line of defense against customer abuse. Every traditional firm also has a compliance department, staffed with people whose task is detecting and preventing that abuse. However, compliance investigations usually begin with the department asking the broker and the manager to tell their version of the alleged abuse. When the broker and the manager—both of whom have an interest in the broker's continued employment—dispute the customer's allegations, you can guess which side the compliance department believes.

If you are younger, better educated, and healthier than Mrs. Pitera, you might be tempted to believe that no broker could ever hurt you by doing the kind of rampant unauthorized trading that Toussaint did in the Piteras' accounts. Don't be so sure. Even well-educated investors are often victims.

Unauthorized trading often occurs because many investors are under the misconception that industry rules permit a broker to place a trade without first getting the customer's permission. Except in clearly defined situations, that is just not the case.

You can give your broker advance permission to place trades without clearing them with you first. This is called giving the broker *discretion* or *discretionary authority*. But this is not something that you can do verbally. There is paperwork that you must sign to grant that authority.

Unauthorized trading happens because, like you and me, brokers have bills to pay. They know how much they have to generate in commissions to cover those bills or to qualify for one of the incentive awards—a cruise, a trip to a luxury resort, and so on—that the firm uses to motivate its sales force. If the end of the month is approaching and they have not reached that number, they may consider unauthorized trading. They know that they can reach their commission goal if they place a few more trades. If they know that you are out of town, in the hospital, preoccupied with work or a family emergency, or just inexperienced in dealing with stockbrokers, they might place a trade in your account without calling you first, figuring that it is easier to get forgiveness than to get permission.

Unauthorized trading is not just a firing offense. It is also an offense that can get a broker kicked out of the securities industry entirely. Why do many brokers take the risk? Because they know that they are likely to get away with it.

Brokers who are inclined to trade without your permission will usually just dip a toe into that water before they jump in. They will buy a stock without talking to you about it first and gauge your reaction. You will not know about the trade until a slip of paper called a *trade confirmation* arrives at your house or you notice the trade when you are looking at your account online. When you do notice it, if you are laboring under the misconception that industry rules allow it, you may not say anything. If the broker does not hear from you, she may be emboldened to begin buying and selling without authorization more often, knowing that as long as the unauthorized trades make you money, you are unlikely to complain.

If you know that your broker is not supposed to trade without your permission, you will call him when you learn about the trade. You'll complain that the broker did not get your permission for the trade. The broker will respond that he had to act quickly to get you the stock at a low price in advance of a sure bump up in the price because of some market or company development. If the stock has risen in value since the purchase, you face a dilemma, and the broker knows it. Do you insist on reversal of the trade and forgo the profit? Or do you accept the trade, sell the stock, and reap the profit? Most investors accept the trade and reap the profit. Of course, the broker reaps the commission. Here is where you must be on your guard. The broker may then tell you that sometimes he is going to see opportunities and will not be able to reach you. The broker will ask whether you want him to act on those opportunities. Many investors will say yes, not knowing that the broker is required to get formal written permission for that kind of authority.

If the stock has dropped in value between the unauthorized purchase and your phone call with the broker, you will insist that the broker reverse the trade. The broker will use all of his sales power to convince you to hold on to the stock, telling you that it is sure to rise in the days that follow. He will suggest that you watch the stock for a couple of weeks and see what happens, promising that you are going to be pleased with the results. Many investors will agree. Others may ask what happens if the broker is wrong and the stock tanks.

This is where the conversation will take a turn for the worse. The broker may say that if the stock tanks, he will pay for the loss himself, which is a serious violation of Financial Industry Regulatory Authority (FINRA)[4] rules. The broker knows that he is unlikely to ever have to make good on that promise. But the broker has to convince you to let the trade stand, or he will be fired. He will say anything to get you to accept the trade. I have seen several cases in which the broker begged the investor not to tell the branch manager.

If you do not report the unauthorized trade in writing as soon as you first notice it, regardless of whether or not the trade has generated a profit, you are setting yourself up for a big loss. What goes up usually comes down, and when the stock goes through the floor, you will call on your broker to make the loss good. The broker will tell you that he cannot do so, and you will finally push past all of the broker's begging and call the branch manager.

Here is where the scene turns ugly. When the manager asks about the trade, the broker will deny the whole affair, saying that you approved the trade. Don't be shocked. If the broker was unethical enough to place an unauthorized trade, he will have no qualms about lying about it. And, of course, the broker knows that his job is on the line. Although the firm will investigate, it will eventually send you a letter denying your claim.

Unless the loss is big enough, pursuing the case further can cost you more than the amount of the loss. Attorneys' fees and filing fees threaten to eat up any recovery. If the loss is big enough to make the expense of pursuing it worthwhile, when the case comes to trial, the defense attorney will cross-examine you.

"This trade occurred on June 1, correct?" the broker's attorney will ask.

"Yes."

"You found out about it on June 2, right?"

"Yes."

"You have testified that you did not approve the trade, correct?"

"I did not approve the trade."

"Yet you did not call the branch manager or complain to anyone about the trade on June 2, did you?"

"I complained to the broker."

"So you say."

"I did."

"That will be for the panel to decide. What we do know is that you did not call the branch manager until September 15, correct?"

"That is correct."

"If the stock had increased in value, we would not be here today, would we?"

". . ."

"Isn't it true that the only reason we are here today is because this stock lost money?"

". . ."

"And you would gladly have accepted the profits if the stock had increased in value. Correct?"

You can see the picture the defense attorney is painting. Because you did not complain to the branch manager immediately, the attorney will be able to make you look like a disgruntled investor who is only trying to avoid the consequences of a bad stock pick.

The vigilant investor knows that unauthorized trading indicates an unethical broker. Whether the trade is profitable or unprofitable, you must complain in writing to the branch manager and to FINRA immediately.[5] Do not be swayed by your broker's begging and/or tears. Report the unauthorized trade. Insist that it be reversed, and begin looking for a new broker. If you delay, the firm will be able to make you look not only like a disgruntled investor, but like a greedy, malicious misanthrope who is willing to destroy a good broker's career to recoup a few thousand dollars.

Of course, reporting an unauthorized trade requires knowing

about it in the first place. People are busy and sometimes leave mail from their brokerage firm unopened. For most investors, the well-known corporate logo on the envelope is enough to inspire confidence that everything is on the up-and-up. Vigilant investors open any mail from their brokerage firm the day they receive it. What they find inside might be benign. But it might be ticking.

If every victim of unauthorized trading were to report it immediately, the investing public could drive out hundreds—perhaps thousands—of bad brokers before they have a chance to ruin the retirements of thousands of other investors. Report unauthorized trades immediately and in writing.

While the Cat's Away: Remote Supervision

David McMillan was a broker for Royal Alliance Associates, Inc., now a subsidiary of insurance giant AIG. McMillan operated out of a one-man office in Bullhead City, Arizona. His supervisor worked 200 miles away in Phoenix.

From 1999 to October 2005, McMillan operated a Ponzi scheme out of his office, defrauding 28 customers of more than $3 million. He told his customers that he was investing their money in securities; however, he was actually spending most of it and sending the rest to earlier investors to maintain the illusion of legitimacy. For six years, McMillan's supervisor failed to detect the con, although a simple review of McMillan's bank records would have uncovered it. Had McMillan had a supervisor on-site, the scam might not have lasted six months.

In April 2009, the SEC fined Royal Alliance $500,000 for failing to detect McMillan's fraud. That was not the first time that the SEC had tagged the firm for poor supervision. In 1997, the SEC had found Royal Alliance's policies insufficient to detect frauds run from one-man offices in Greensboro, North Carolina, and Cocoa Beach, Florida. Those cons cost investors more than $1 million. Royal Alliance settled each of those SEC actions without admitting or denying the SEC's allegations.

Royal Alliance is an independent broker-dealer. It and other independent firms, like LPL Financial, Ameriprise Financial, and Raymond James Financial, offer brokers who want to flee the produce-or-get-canned environment in boiler rooms and traditional firms a different business model. Independent brokers cover their own business expenses and, in return, receive a much larger percentage of the commission from each trade. Rather than reporting to an office with the brokerage firm's name on the door and a branch manager looking over their shoulder, brokers at independent firms lease their own office, hire their own staff, and select their own name for their business. There is no supervisor on-site.

The independent model, which allows for remote supervision, presents challenges that anyone can understand. A rogue broker without a supervisor within 100 miles does not have to be as concerned about being caught as a broker who is working in the same office as her supervisor, however lax that individual might be (while the cat's away . . .). The vigilant investor who uses a broker supervised by an independent firm finds out where his broker's supervisor is and considers how closely the supervisor can reasonably monitor the broker from that distance. The vigilant investor also investigates the firm's record of supervision, or lack thereof, through a CRD report from the state securities commissioner.

Because independent brokers usually create their own business names, it is often not immediately obvious what firm the broker is associated with. But somewhere in the broker's promotional materials or on an account statement will be a sentence that begins, "Securities offered through . . ." The rest of that sentence identifies the firm that is supposed to be supervising the broker.

Image Is Everything

As a pitchman for Canon cameras, Andre Agassi famously said, "Image is everything." Brokerage firms knew that before Canon's ad agency thought of it. They burn into the public consciousness slogans like "Tradition of Trust" and "We make money the old-fashioned way. We earn it." But the truth is a long way from the image.

Nine-figure marketing budgets allow traditional firms to bombard you with ads portraying them as safe and trustworthy. The advertising does its job. Investors are prone to believe that any firm with an impressive name and a long history is reputable. The financial crisis of 2007–2008 should have taught us differently. But the ads keep coming and will soon erase those misdeeds from our memories.

You can get a sense of this effect by playing a word association game. Morgan Stanley, Smith Barney, Merrill Lynch. When you read those names, what words occur to you? For many readers, the responses are words like *big*, *established*, *stable*, and *reputable*. Few investors remember that the biggest names in the securities industry lied to us about ratings on technology stocks in the early 2000s in order to curry favor with the companies whose stocks they followed. They told us to buy Pets.com, while acknowledging in internal e-mails that the stock was "a dog." They did the same with many other dot-com companies. But when it comes to brokerage firm misconduct, we are all hopeless amnesiacs.

Many investors believe that well-respected firms would be outraged and embarrassed at the mere thought that one of their brokers had taken advantage of a customer. Even people who have prior experience with brokers believe that a large firm will rush to make everything right "to avoid bad publicity." But large brokerage firms get so many complaints about brokers mistreating customers that the firms consider them little more than a mild irritant, just another cost of doing business. Bad press regarding how the firm mistreated an investor is no match for the firm's $100 million marketing budget.

I travel the country speaking to groups of all sizes, educating them about investment fraud and how to spot it. After most of those talks, at least one person approaches me and asks a variation of this question: "My money is at [Well-Known Brokerage Firm]. So, I'm okay, right?" My answer is always the same. "Not necessarily." The vigilant investor is not impressed by advertising, plush offices, or familiar names.

Investment fraud happens at all types of brokerage firms, and it's getting worse. In 2009, 16 percent of financial fraud cases brought by the SEC involved registered brokerage firms, up from 9 percent in 2008. Remember that, unlike the stock market, fraud never slumps, and much of that fraud happens at brokerage firms.

Due Diligence for the Vigilant

The vigilant investor:

➤ Checks a broker's performance on licensing examinations through a CRD report

➤ Hangs up on boiler room cold calls

▶ Checks sec.gov and the CRD report to find out whether a broker has been kicked out of the securities industry

▶ Complains in writing about unauthorized trading immediately, no matter how small the trade and whether the trade was profitable or not

▶ Opens mail from her brokerage firm immediately

▶ Investigates where his broker's supervisor is located and researches the firm's supervisory record at sec.gov and through a CRD report on the firm

▶ Pays no attention to image, but remembers that firms of all types, from boiler rooms to the biggest names on Wall Street, have been guilty of customer abuse

8

Managing Mavericks

Knowing How Compliance Systems Work
Can Help You Protect Your Nest Egg

Education is when you read the fine print; experience is what
you get when you don't.

—Pete Seeger

In 2000, Howard "Buck" McHugh was a hit with senior management
at broker-dealer A.G. Edwards & Sons, Inc. (AGE). He was a big
producer, one who was always at or near the top of the production
list. According to his customers, McHugh generated those commissions by churning the accounts of blue-collar retirees from Boston
Edison Company (Boston Ed), a New England electric service pro-
vider. When McHugh's supervisor tried to stop the misconduct, upper
management intervened and allowed him to continue generating large
commissions at the expense of the retirees.

McHugh's story illustrates the continual tension between supervisory and compliance personnel, who are supposed to keep customers safe, and upper management, which is more concerned with the bottom line. In this chapter, we will look at that tension and see how the industry protects brokers whom it knows to be dangerous. We will also explore the mechanics of how compliance personnel identify broker misconduct, and how a vigilant investor can use that knowledge to better protect her nest egg. Finally, we'll see how the seemingly innocuous paperwork associated with any brokerage account can help us identify an unethical broker.

Profits Above People

Before its 2007 merger with Wachovia Securities, Inc., A.G. Edwards had a proud tradition of independence.[1] Founded in 1887 in St. Louis by Albert Gallatin Edwards, it was the first St. Louis firm to have a seat on the New York Stock Exchange (NYSE). With offices in every state, as well as in London and Geneva, AGE was a traditional brokerage firm with a better than average reputation for broker supervision. But that was before Buck McHugh showed up.

In 1996, McHugh was 28 and hungry. He wanted to make his mark at AGE, and he had a plan. Boston Ed had announced that it was reducing its workforce by several hundred people and was offering early retirement buyouts. McHugh had a list of prospective Boston Ed retirees, each of whom had a pension plan account that the individual had been paying into for 30 years or more.

McHugh cold-called the retiring Boston Ed workers, pressured them into opening accounts with AGE, and recommended that they take their retirement benefits in a lump sum rather than as a lifetime annuity. McHugh's cold calling and sales techniques were so aggressive that they drew the attention of Boston Ed's chairman of the board, Thomas May. Seeking to protect his former workers, May placed an insert in the electric bills of all Boston Ed employees warning them away from McHugh by name. It didn't work.

Fred Gennelly was McHugh's branch manager in the Plymouth, Massachusetts, office, where McHugh began his AGE career. Noticing McHugh's aggressive sales techniques, he told McHugh to stop cold-calling Boston Ed retirees. McHugh ignored him. Gennelly then wrote a memorandum to McHugh's personnel file documenting the directive and notifying McHugh that he would be fired immediately if he continued to cold-call Boston Ed retirees. McHugh was asked to sign it, but he refused.

To escape scrutiny, McHugh left the Plymouth AGE office and moved 40 miles up the road to the Boston branch office, where he continued cold-calling Boston Ed retirees and racking up branch-leading commission totals. When McHugh transferred, Gennelly called Gerald Buckley, the Boston branch manager, to say that McHugh "needed some mentoring." But he did not tell Buckley about McHugh's treatment of Boston Ed retirees. Buckley soon had reason to suspect that McHugh had more than the usual need to generate large commissions. In December 1998, one of McHugh's creditors filed a garnishment action to collect a portion of McHugh's AGE paychecks in payment of a judgment arising from an unpaid debt.

Buckley began to see the same activity that had led Gennelly to issue an ultimatum to McHugh. There was excessive trading in the accounts of elderly Boston Ed retirees, one of whom had called Buckley to complain. In December 1999, Michael Caputo, the experienced broker whom Buckley had assigned to mentor McHugh, reported unnecessary trading in the retirees' accounts that was costing them more than $1,700 per month.

McHugh never understood why he received criticism (rather than praise) for generating such impressive commission totals. He felt unduly constrained by Buckley, and he resented having Caputo looking over his shoulder. Deciding to complain up the chain of command, McHugh wrote a letter to Buckley's supervisor, AGE Regional Manager Bill Branson, detailing his complaints about Buckley and Caputo.

Branson scheduled a trip to the Boston office in the summer of 2000 to address the situation. It didn't go as Buckley and Caputo expected. Branson insulted Caputo, insinuated that he was trying to steal McHugh's Boston Ed customers, and ended the meeting by telling Buckley to "take it easy" on McHugh. Caputo quit the following day. In his testimony before the Massachusetts Securities Commission, which filed an enforcement action against AGE arising from McHugh's conduct, Branson defended his decision to ease management's scrutiny of McHugh. He testified that he did not believe that McHugh needed a mentor, saying, "Buck was past that, *his production was substantial, it might have been one of the highest in the office, I mean, it was a large number*" (emphasis added).

Buckley was so disturbed by the meeting with Branson that he wrote a letter to AGE's director of branch offices, Robert Bagby—who, less than one year later, would become the CEO and chairman of AGE—raising concern about his ability to supervise McHugh in light of Branson's instruction to "take it easy." The letter had no effect. Buckley testified that he did not believe that Bagby took his concerns seriously.

McHugh went back to generating commissions from Boston Ed customers. A few months later, he left AGE for the less intense supervision of independent broker LPL Financial.

Upper management's single-minded focus on the bottom line

showed itself again when McHugh's customers asked AGE to repay the money that he had cost them. Rather than making McHugh's customers whole, AGE took a tough negotiating stance with each of them and succeeded in negotiating settlements of less than 50 percent of the claimed losses in most cases.

McHugh's scenario plays itself out hundreds—if not thousands—of times every year at brokerage firms all over the country. Supervisors and compliance department employees who are responsible for ensuring the safety of customers dutifully report apparent misconduct. But when the broker is a big producer, the people who are responsible for maximizing the firm's bottom line often tell the compliance people to "back off."

No one has identified the problem better than Lori Richards, the head of the SEC's Office of Compliance Inspections and Examinations from 1995 to 2009. In a 2007 speech to a meeting of the National Society of Compliance Professionals, Ms. Richards said:

> A common example . . . is firm[s] that allow excessive deference to their big producers, and to avoid alienating the big producer, managers don't really want to know how he got that way. In this environment, a compliance person who reaches in to find out why the big producer is such a big producer may face pushback and even hostility. . . . Lack of real support by senior management is far and away the fastest and most destructive retardant to an effective compliance program. It's pretty easy for employees to see when the firm's leaders are paying lip service to the importance of compliance.

The vigilant investor looks into a firm's reputation for supervision. While FINRA's BrokerCheck is worse than useless for investigating individual brokers, it is better at reporting on regulatory actions against brokerage firms. Go to www.finra.org and select the link for

BrokerCheck. It will allow you to search for a brokerage firm. Pay special attention to regulatory actions alleging "failure to supervise." More than anything else, failure to supervise violations reveal a culture that puts profits above people.

Remember that garnishment action filed against McHugh by an unpaid creditor? It's likely that none of McHugh's customers ever knew about it. But a vigilant investor knows that signs of financial distress indicate a powerful motivation for misconduct. You can investigate your broker's financial history by searching PACER for bankruptcy filings and federal lawsuits, and state courthouses for lawsuits by creditors.

Letting the Lions Roar Without Their Feasting on the Audience

Branch managers and compliance personnel have an impossible job, and it's no wonder that they fail as often as they succeed. Like lion tamers in a circus, they have to restrain the very thing that makes the show worth seeing. A lion who looks no more dangerous than a kitten won't sell tickets, and a broker whose primary goal is avoiding the smallest infraction of the rules won't sell as many investments. The SEC has delegated to FINRA the job of keeping the lions from mauling the audience, and FINRA has delegated that job to the brokerage firms, who count on branch managers and compliance personnel to detect and prevent broker misconduct. It's a big job.

Billions of stock trades take place on American securities exchanges every trading day. Even an army of branch managers could not possibly scrutinize every trade, so brokerage firms use computers to help them identify broker misconduct. The computers are programmed to identify accounts that exceed certain parameters (more than so many trades in a month, more than a certain percentage of assets in a single stock, and so on). Don't be comforted by this. Humans often thwart the computer's good work in identifying possible misconduct. Branch managers in a firm that, in Lori Richards's words, "pay[s] lip service to the importance of compliance" know that restraining a big producer is no ticket to advancement.

When a computer in the firm's compliance department identifies an account in which there might be broker misconduct, it spits out a report called an *exception report* or an *activity report*. The report is then sent to the branch manager of the office where the account is located.

Now that you're more than halfway through your training to become a vigilant investor, you know what the branch manager *should* do with the exception report. The manager should call the customer to attempt to discover whether there has actually been any broker misconduct. But the branch manager does not necessarily *want* to learn of broker misconduct. The broker makes the firm and the manager a lot of money, so the branch manager may want to avoid learning of anything that could threaten the broker's continued employment. "Besides," the manager might think, "a phone call like that might spook the customer and lead her to move her account to another firm, even if the broker did nothing wrong."

So instead of going to the best source (the customer), the branch manager asks the broker for an explanation of the trading activity identified in the report. Of course, the broker will have an explanation: "It was all the customer's idea." The branch manager will report that explanation to the compliance department, and that is where the matter will end. The customer will never know that his account was flagged for possible broker misconduct. If you think the procedure seems designed specifically *not* to find the conduct that led the computer to flag the account, you're right. Which is why you must be vigilant.

A Happiness Letter Is No Reason for Celebration

Sometimes a firm's rules *require* the branch manager to contact the customer regarding possible misconduct. A letter that was actually designed to discover broker misconduct would read something like this: "Dear Customer: I'm concerned that your trading is riskier than it should be, given your investment objectives and risk tolerance. The broker tells me that all these trades were your idea. If that is not the case, please call me right away."

While the branch manager may prefer not to write such a letter, if she does not write *some kind* of letter, she will get in trouble for not complying with written policies. So the branch manager technically complies with the firm's policy (without any intention of really discovering misconduct) by writing a "happiness letter," so called because it appears to be nothing more than a customer relations initiative designed to make sure that the customer is happy. The letter, which expresses how pleased the branch manager is to have the customer's business and reminds him she is "always available" if he has any questions or concerns, is so innocuous that the customer may think that it's being sent to every client. Having read the letter, the customer might feel relieved to think that the branch manager has his best interest in mind. He'll have no idea that the firm's compliance system has identified what may be broker misconduct.

The happiness letter is a cynical ploy to set a customer up in the event of a dispute about the conduct that prompted the letter. At the trial of the customer's dispute with the broker and the firm, the firm's attorney will wave the letter around and establish that the customer received it. She will establish that the customer did not call the branch manager when he received the letter. The attorney will then argue that the customer must have been pleased with the broker's activity or he would have taken the manager up on her invitation to call. Naturally, the letter is so vague that only a vigilant investor will recognize it as a signal that something is wrong.

If you receive a happiness letter from your branch manager, call the manager and ask what exception report your account appeared on and what that report is designed to detect. In addition, confirm the value of your account as it appears on your last monthly statement. You might learn that you've been receiving phony statements. Inform the branch manager of any trades in your account in the last month, and tell him which trades the broker suggested. Follow up with an e-mail documenting the conversation. Branch managers tend to have lousy memories of these sorts of discussions.

Be on your guard against one other tactic of the willfully blind branch manager as well. Sometimes, when she receives a call from a worried customer, the branch manager will refer the customer back to the broker. That's like a teacher referring a student back to the bully who has been tormenting him. If a branch manager says, "Talk to the broker," the vigilant investor confirms that conversation in writing and goes looking for another firm.

Account-Opening Documents: The Most Important Boring Forms You May Ever Sign

Every firm has volumes of rules and regulations that govern what brokers can and can't do, and what a broker can and can't say to a customer. No investor would find them very interesting. But there are important customer protection policies in those rules. Among them are rules requiring that firms collect paperwork from the customer, paperwork that influences how the broker behaves.

The paperwork begins when you first open a brokerage account. Before you were a vigilant investor, you may have thought of that paperwork as a mere formality, no more significant than the form you fill out to get a library card. But how you complete that paperwork can determine whether you achieve the retirement you've planned for or will have to scrape by on social security.

The information that you give your broker when you open an account will determine how closely the computers in the firm's compliance department will monitor your account. The more investing experience you have, the wealthier you are, the higher your income, and the riskier your investment objectives, the less likely it is that the computers will flag your account. Make sure your broker gets it right when she records your income, investment experience, net worth, investment objectives, and risk tolerance on the account-opening forms. If you're not asked for this information, don't sign the account-opening document and start looking for another broker. The broker who says that all she needs from you to open an account is your signature may intend to take advantage of you by making up information that will lead the computers to ignore you.

A broker has every incentive to make you look like Bill Gates on these documents. The wealthier you are and the more sophisticated you are regarding investments, the fewer questions the branch manager will ask the broker about risky or frequent trading in your account. Brokers can fill in the blanks on the account-opening forms to make it look as if an investor who has never had a brokerage account has 30 years of investment experience, or as if someone who makes $30,000 per year makes $150,000 per year. They can fill in an investor's income *before* he retired, even though he is no longer receiving a salary. Never sign incomplete account-opening paperwork, and get a copy of what you do sign before you leave the broker's office. Keep that paperwork in a safe place. As we'll soon see, you may need it later.

The broker should always ask about your investment objectives—what you want this money to do for you. Different firms use different terms for these objectives, but many firms describe them, from most conservative to most risky, as follows: preservation of principal, income, conservative growth, aggressive growth, and speculation. Unless you're willing to gamble on your future, if you are retiring without a big surplus in your nest egg, you do not want the word *speculation* to appear anywhere in your investment objectives. Also, keep in mind that "aggressive growth" is almost as risky as speculation.

If your brokerage firm asks you to rank your investment objectives in order of priority, unless you want to speculate, refuse to rank speculation anywhere on the list. Your broker might say, "Well, we have to rank them all, so we'll just rank speculation last." Don't agree to this. When push comes to shove and you face your broker in a courtroom or arbitration hearing, the firm will pull out your investment objectives and say, "I see here that you ranked speculation among your investment objectives." "No," you'll say, "I ranked it last because I did not want to speculate." "Well," the defense attorney will reply, "if you did not want to speculate, you could have just not ranked speculation, right?" If the broker insists that you put something in the box next to speculation, write "NO."

This brings us to one of the securities industry's dirtiest little secrets. Given what you know about the industry, you may not be surprised to learn that brokers sometimes change your investment objectives without telling you, almost always making them riskier. In March 2009, FINRA Enforcement fined Wachovia Securities LLC (now Wells Fargo Investments) $1.1 million for failing to notify 300,000 customers of changes in their investment objectives. That is like learning that your doctor did not call you with test results that showed that you have a treatable disease. Who knows what the delay in treatment cost you?

A broker might change your investment objectives without telling you because this makes it easier for her to make more and riskier trades in your account without your account being flagged. While most investors may not uncover such a change until it is too late, the vigilant investor can catch this dirty trick early by reviewing his monthly account statements carefully.

The Evidence in the Mail: Monthly Account Statements and Trade Confirmations

In the previous chapter, we mentioned the importance of opening all of your mail from your brokerage firm. Once a month, you'll receive a statement showing all activity in your account. Just as important as the information regarding the value of your account and the details of what you bought or sold last month is the information about your investment objectives, which will appear somewhere on the statement. Be sure to compare the investment objectives on the account statement with those that you gave the firm when you opened your account. If they don't match, you know that the broker has changed them without your permission. If this happens to you, call the branch manager and ask what exception report your account appeared on recently and what that report aims to detect. Report the unauthorized change to the branch manager and confirm it all in an e-mail. Then file a complaint with FINRA.

Another piece of mail that you will receive from your brokerage firm is more important than you ever realized. It's the trade confirmation that you receive every time the broker places a trade in your account. In addition to helping you spot unauthorized trading (discussed in Chapter 7), the trade confirmation can help you identify a broker who has crossed another ethical line.

The confirmation will show what stock you bought or sold, how many shares, the date, the price, and the commission. In addition, sometimes the confirmation will contain the word *unsolicited*, often abbreviated *unsol*. Unsolicited means that the trade was your idea. If that is not true, the broker is lying to the branch manager about how often you call to place a trade versus how often the broker solicits trades from you.

Why would your broker do that? It could be that she is buying investments that are inconsistent with your objectives and wants to be able to blame you if they go bad. Or it could be that she wants to make it look as if you are a sophisticated investor who spends all of his time watching CNBC. This way, if there is a dispute, your broker will be able to make it appear that you never relied upon her advice, but kept your own counsel. But the reason is less important than the fact of the broker's misrepresentation.

In 2009, FINRA commenced an enforcement action accusing Clint Keener, a broker with Stifel, Nicolaus & Company, Inc., in Mansfield, Ohio, of unsuitably risky trading in the accounts of a 60-year-old couple with no previous investment experience. According to FINRA, Keener mismarked trades, for this couple and for other customers, as unsolicited. Doing so made it less likely that Keener's firm would have questioned him about the unusual trading. In July 2010, Keener consented to be suspended from the securities industry for two months without admitting or denying FINRA's allegations. As of this writing, Keener is back in the industry with a new firm, having served his suspension.

In 2009, FINRA began an enforcement action against Eugene Roesser, Jr., a broker at Merrill Lynch in North Potomac, Maryland, for allegedly mismarking customer trades as unsolicited and for discretionary trading in customers' accounts without their written authorization. Roesser, like Keener, consented to a suspension from the securities industry without admitting or denying the allegations. He was fined $15,000 and suspended for only three weeks.

Keener and Roesser have plenty of company. Each month, FINRA produces a list of firms and brokers who have been suspended or barred from the industry. Mismarking customer orders and filling in incorrect information on account-opening documents appear frequently in the charges. In 2010 alone, FINRA suspended or barred 644 brokers for unethical conduct. Most of them are back in the industry with their customers none the wiser.

If a broker is trying to make a solicited trade look unsolicited, he is being unethical. The vigilant investor will fire that broker before he strays even further into unethical territory. Again, it is important that you report the mischaracterization of a trade immediately and in writing. Not only will you be saving your nest egg from more serious damage, but you'll be helping to shorten the career of a broker whose lack of ethics might otherwise harm hundreds of other investors.

Controlling the Rogue Lion: "Special Supervision"

Firms don't like to lose productive brokers. And FINRA, although it has a committed and hardworking enforcement staff, is a trade group that is made up exclusively of brokerage firms. So FINRA allows firms to keep even lions that have leapt into the audience and done some damage there by placing those brokers on what is called "special supervision." You can think of it as putting another lion tamer in with the productive but unruly broker.

Brokers who are under special supervision must get prior approval from their branch manager for every trade they make. They must also endure more scrutiny from their manager than other brokers. However, the daily crush of a branch manager's duties means that special supervision is often not so special.

Despite the lion tamer's most fervent hopes, a lion that has escaped into the audience once is more likely to do so again. The vigilant investor avoids the rogue lion by using FINRA's rules and asking a broker's branch manager whether the broker has ever been under special supervision. If the manager says no, confirm that answer in an e-mail to the manager. If the manager answers yes, find another broker.

Due Diligence for the Vigilant

The vigilant investor:

▶ Understands that a brokerage firm will protect a big producer and side with the broker over the investor

▶ Investigates a firm's record of broker supervision via FINRA's BrokerCheck

▶ Investigates, via PACER and state courthouse records, whether his broker has financial difficulties that might motivate her to misconduct

▶ If he receives a "happiness letter," asks the branch manager what exception report his account has appeared on and what that report is designed to detect

▶ Finds another firm if the branch manager responds to complaints by saying, "Talk to the broker"

▶ Makes sure that the broker fills in the correct information on account-opening documents and keeps a copy of that paperwork in a safe place

▶ Reviews her monthly account statements to confirm that the firm has not changed her account objectives

▶ Reviews trade confirmations and reports any trades that are mismarked as unsolicited to the branch manager, immediately and in writing

▶ Asks his broker's branch manager whether the broker has ever been under special supervision, and confirms the answer in writing

9

Sales Scripts, Bullets, and the One-Two Punch

A Peek into the Stockbrokers' Bag of Tricks

The salesman knows nothing of what he is selling save that
he is charging a great deal too much for it.

—Oscar Wilde

In a November 1993 article entitled "Money Angles Miracle on Wall Street!" *Time* magazine covered a new development in the brokerage business: Detroit-based brokerage firm Olde Discount Corp. was offering no-commission stock trades. It was a deal that not even the E*TRADE Baby could have matched. But less than five years later, in September 1998, the SEC fined Olde Discount $4 million; barred its national sales director and a regional manager from the securities industry; and fined the founder of the firm, Ernest J. Olde, $1 million.

Olde Discount was not the kind of "discount" broker that waits for its customers' instructions. The firm used draconian production quotas to motivate its inexperienced brokers to pressure customers to buy risky stocks that it recommended. The profits placed Ernest Olde on the Forbes 400 list of the wealthiest people in America four times in the 1990s. Perhaps appreciating how much the SEC had permanently cramped Olde Discount's style, Ernest Olde sold his company to H&R Block for $850 million in cash within a few months of the SEC's action, renounced his U.S. citizenship, and moved to the Cayman Islands. H&R Block made a run at the brokerage business, operating it under the name H&R Block Financial Advisers until 2008, when it sold the business to Ameriprise Financial for $315 million in cash, more than half a billion dollars less than it had paid for the company.

The sales techniques that made Olde Discount so profitable in the 1990s are still in use today at firms of all types—boiler rooms, independents, and traditional firms—because they work. In this chapter, we will look at several of those tricks of the trade, discuss why they are so effective, and equip the vigilant investor to defend herself against them.

Stick to the Script

Olde Discount recruited new brokers right out of college. To quickly discover whether a candidate had any hope of success in the firm's system, in the first interview, the recruiter would give the candidate a research report on a particular stock, tell him to study it for 10 minutes, and then have him pitch the stock to the recruiter. Those who performed well got hired. Those who were prepared only for a where-do-you-see-yourself-in-five-years interview got rejected.

Like all brokerage firms, once its new recruits passed the Series 7 exam, Olde Discount sent them to a several-week training session at company headquarters. More than 90 percent of the time was spent on sales training, teaching the recruits how to convince a customer to buy an investment that paid Olde Discount and the broker a big commission. The firm called those stocks "special venture stocks"; they were issued by risky start-up companies that its research department followed.

Olde Discount gave its new recruits scripts that helped them sell special venture stocks even to customers who had called to purchase something else. The firm's commission structure paid brokers next to nothing for anything other than special venture stocks, so every broker understood immediately the importance of learning the scripts. The "cross-selling" scripts had the names of stocks that customers frequently wanted to buy on one side of the page, and the alternative special venture stocks on the other. If a customer called with an order for IBM stock, the broker could find IBM on the list, slide her finger over to the other side of the page, and find the special venture stock of a start-up computer company that the broker was to pressure the customer to buy instead. The Olde Discount mindset was so pervasive that its regional manager, Dan Katzman, testified (to yours truly) during the SEC's investigation of the firm, "Why let someone buy a stock you are not going to get paid on?"

Olde Discount provided other scripts to its new recruits as well. Perhaps the most helpful was a script that listed every possible objection that a customer might offer in resisting the broker's high-pressure pitch of a special venture stock. As with the cross-selling scripts, the objection was on the left side of the paper, with the response across from it. To the customer who said that he'd have to check with his wife, the firm's script called for the broker to say, "What if she says no? I'm telling you this idea because I'm an expert. I'm not the final authority, but I make my living doing this. I hope the person you check with cares as much about your financial success as I do." To the objection, "I'll watch the stock for a while," the script required the brokers to say, "You'll only watch it go up. I've been watching this stock for two years. This is the time to buy 1,000 shares." Because of Olde Discount's high turnover rate, there were few, if any, brokers who had actually been in the securities industry for two years, much less followed a specific special venture stock for that long.

To chisel the scripts into the trainees' minds, Olde Discount had them pair up and role-play. One trainee was the broker; the other was the reluctant customer. The broker tried to sell the stock. The customer resisted, offering objection after objection for the broker to overcome. The exercise continued, day after day, until the responses became second nature.

Brokers learn sales scripts like Cub Scouts learn the Pledge of Allegiance. Your broker has a sales script like Olde Discount's or has long ago memorized such a script. The training that your broker received at the beginning of her career was more like Olde Discount's training than the broker would like you to know.

Smart salespeople in every industry think of possible objections and are prepared to respond to them. And scripts can be a smart way for a company to make sure that salespeople are not "winging it" or making promises that go beyond what the product can deliver. But your broker is not selling timeshares or soliciting a contribution to your alma mater. The broker is addressing something that is profoundly more important than a week in Panama City or the size of your school's endowment: your financial security. Scripted sales tactics and a secure retirement go together like cyclones and Bangladesh.

The vigilant investor stays attuned to how his broker responds to concerns about a recommendation. Next time your broker calls with a recommendation, resist it. Try the old "I'll have to check with my spouse" objection and see how the broker responds. It's a reasonable objection. Does the broker respect it, or does she have a ready response that seems to dispose of the objection? You want a broker who listens, not an actor who can deliver lines as well as Meryl Streep.

Vigilant investors also pay attention to where their broker learned the securities business. Was it at a notorious firm like Stratton Oakmont or Olde Discount? The CRD from your state securities regulator will give you the broker's employment history. A Google search that includes the name of the broker's first firm and "SEC" or "FINRA"[1] will bring up news stories about major regulatory actions. Read them to find out whether the regulator accused the firm of high-pressure sales tactics, churning, or unauthorized trading. If the results are troubling, see how long your broker spent at that firm. A stay of three months is little cause for concern. A year or more at such a firm indicates that the broker may have bought into its culture of customer abuse and ingrained bad habits.

While you are reviewing the CRD, pay attention to how long a broker spent at each of his other previous employers. Several stays of less than two years might indicate that he has difficulty complying with a firm's customer protection policies and procedures. You don't want a maverick. You want a rule follower. Ask the broker why he has worked at so many different firms for such a short time.

Brokers are salespeople, plain and simple. They call themselves "financial advisers," but that is like a car salesman calling himself your transportation adviser or a grocery store clerk calling herself your nutritional adviser. In the words of Warren Buffett, "The broker is not your friend. He's more like a doctor who charges patients on how often they change medicines."

Three Bullets and a Close

Olde Discount trained its brokers on a technique called "three bullets and a close." Your broker knows this technique. The key is to create a sense of urgency. The broker wants her tone of voice to paint a mental picture of a quickly evaporating opportunity to purchase a priceless asset at a bargain basement price. With that excitement in her voice, the broker gives you three positive facts (the bullets) about the stock, and then asks you for the order (the close).

The three-bullets pitch sounds like this:

> **Pat, Hi. Jane Dollar here. I've got a terrific opportunity for us. It's Banana, Inc. They are announcing earnings today, and we anticipate that they will be better than what the Street is expecting (bullet 1), their product is high in potassium (bullet 2), and the bad weather in South America means that the supply is going to be limited this year, so prices will rise (bullet 3). Let's pick up 500 shares (the close).**

Some firms train their brokers never to take no for an answer. If you object to buying Banana, Inc., the broker will give you three more bullets and another close. "The product is delicious (bullet 1), monkeys love them (bullet 2), and the surgeon general recommends eating at least two a day (bullet 3). Let's get those 500 shares while we can still get them at this price (close)." Boiler room firms train their brokers to keep going with this technique until you either agree or hang up.

Notice the use of "let's" in the sentence, "Let's pick up 500 shares." The broker phrases the close that way for a reason: It puts the broker on your side of the fence. Thereafter, the call seems not so much like a sales pitch as like friendly advice from a trusted partner. The vigilant investor is not pulled in by that tactic. Whenever you hear your broker use the words *we*, *us*, or *let's*, ask yourself whose money the broker will be using to buy the investment and who, alone, will suffer the loss if the investment tanks.

No Money? No Problem

On one of Olde Discount's scripts, across from the objection "I don't have any money" was "Explain the benefits of margin." If you have had a brokerage account for any length of time, you have heard your broker refer to margin. *Margin* is a loan that the brokerage firm gives you to allow you to buy more stock. Your broker loves margin. It enables the broker to sell you twice as many shares for the money you have available. More to the point, the broker can generate twice the commissions and supplement his income with a cut of the monthly interest that you pay.

Brokerages love margin so much that they give their brokers continually updated information about the maximum that each customer can borrow from the firm. When your broker looks at your account, she sees not only the securities, but also a number called *buying power*. Buying power is nothing more than the dollars that you could borrow if you were margined to the hilt. Your broker knows the buying power of your account and thinks of unused margin as a missed opportunity.

The margin loan is secured by the investments in your account. If the value of the investments declines, the collateral that secures the loan loses value. Imagine how your mortgage company would feel if bedrooms or bathrooms began disappearing from your house. Suddenly there is a loan of $200,000 secured by a house that is worth only $100,000. Unlike your mortgage company, though, a brokerage firm can force the sale of your investments for no reason other than that the value of the collateral is shrinking. Every brokerage has an official level of discomfort with the evaporation of collateral, after which it will insist that you give it additional collateral (such as other stocks) or pay down the margin loan. The industry calls the request for additional collateral a *margin call*, but that term is really a sophisticated way of saying that it's time for a fire sale.

Because the drop in the stock price was the event that triggered the demand for more collateral, you will have to sell the stocks at the lowest price they have reached since you owned them. Few things are certain with the stock market, but selling at the bottom to meet a margin call is a sure thing.

Sometimes brokerage firms offer fee-based accounts rather than commission-based accounts. With a fee-based account, the firm does not charge for each trade, but instead takes a percentage of the value of the account each month. Firms use margin to increase what they make off you even in those accounts.

The fine print of the account-opening agreement for a fee-based account spells out how the firm will calculate the monthly fee. Most such agreements say that the firm calculates the fee using the value of the investments in the account. That sounds reasonable enough, right? But what if you have a margin loan that has financed the purchase of half of those investments? In most cases, the firm ignores the margin loan! If you have an account with $200,000 in stocks and a $100,000 margin loan, the net value of the account is $100,000. But when the firm calculates the fee that you owe, it calculates it on

$200,000, not the $100,000 that the account is really worth. You wind up paying twice the fee of someone who owns a $100,000 account with no margin debt.

Having a margin account requires a level of continual attention that few investors have the time to give. The vigilant investor avoids margin unless he can afford to devote that much time and understands that things can go south faster and farther than temperatures in Fargo.

The One-Two Punch

The savvy broker knows that you've been warned against buying stocks from boiler room salespeople. She therefore uses a technique that I call the *one-two punch* to make herself seem more like a trusted adviser who wants to "partner" in your financial success and less like a commission-hungry salesperson.

A broker will cold-call prospects from a list of leads (perhaps subscribers to a financial magazine). The broker will introduce herself and quickly say, "I am not selling anything." The rest of the pitch goes something like this:

"I just noticed your name on a list of successful businesspeople, and I thought I would call and introduce myself and ask whether you might be interested in opportunities for quick profits should they come across my screen."

"What kind of opportunities?" you ask.

"Stocks that are poised for a sharp rise," the broker will respond. "There's nothing like that available right now," the broker will say, "but every now and then we see a sure winner, a chance for a big, quick profit. Would you be interested in hearing from me if I come across something like that?"

You can appreciate the subtlety of this pitch. The broker is not selling anything. She doesn't want anything from you except permission to call if she can make you some quick money. *Why not?* you think. Like most investors, you give the broker permission to call if she finds a great opportunity.

The broker is trained to wait a week or two, long enough that the setup is not obvious, but not so long that you will have forgotten your first conversation. But the broker *will* call again.

"Hi, Mr. Huddleston. This is Missy Turnover. We spoke last week. A great opportunity just popped up on my screen, and I thought of you. Do you have 30 seconds for me to tell you about it?"

Here is where the setup pays off. She did not try to sell you anything the first time around. She did not call you back immediately. And she thought of you—captain of industry that you are—when a chance to make some quick money came up. The setup and the subtle flattery can be hard to resist.

Of course, the "great opportunity" is just another stock. The broker has no reason to suspect that it is going to shoot through the roof. She could have tried to sell it to you in her first call. But making the pitch in two stages has given her more credibility. You have given her permission to call you, thus elevating her above the half-dozen unsolicited sales calls that you get in an average day. The wait after the first call has made you believe that she really has been waiting to find a stock that can make you some quick money.

When the broker throws the first punch in the one-two combination, the vigilant investor steps forward and delivers a jab of, "No, thank you. Don't call again." If the broker is willing to deceive you by suggesting in the first call that there is nothing that he would like you to buy, you don't want to get the second call.

The broker won't go down easily. He will keep swinging, trying to engage you in conversation with a question such as, "You don't like to make money?" The broker knows that the longer he can keep you talking, the better his chances of delivering a knockout blow. At that moment, the vigilant investor throws the haymaker—"Nope"—and hangs up.

Silence and Slippery Answers

While every brokerage firm has a commission schedule that outlines the standard charges for the purchase of different types of securities (stocks, bonds, options, and so on), your broker has not told you that she can discount the commissions. The trick here is for the broker to keep her mouth shut about that fact. And, indeed, why would the broker forgo earning the maximum commission by telling you such a thing? To answer that question, think back to your initial meeting with the broker. Unless the meeting was unusual, the broker gave you the impression that she would give anything short of her child's kidney to help you meet your financial goals. Now try to square that with your broker's deliberately keeping quiet about your being entitled to give her less of your money.

Some of your broker's customers never pay what's printed on the official commission schedule. They ask for, and routinely receive, a discount from the published schedule. Why don't you get those discounts? Because you haven't asked. If your account is small and your demands on the broker's time are great, he might refuse you that discount, figuring that it's not worth the effort to keep your account. But that reaction is rare.

For some investments, like mutual funds that charge a commission and unit investment trusts,[2] the issuer of the securities mandates a volume discount; the commission percentage drops for purchases above a certain dollar figure, typically $25,000. The biggest firms on Wall Street routinely fail to give customers these breakpoint commission discounts. In August 2010, FINRA fined Merrill Lynch $2.5 million for failing to give investors in unit investment trusts breakpoint commission discounts. The vigilant investor checks the web site of the mutual fund company or unit investment trust company for information on breakpoint discounts. If your broker's trades in such securities fall suspiciously below a breakpoint, you need another broker.

Brokers save the most devious sales trick for sales of variable annuities, which are securities issued by insurance companies (more about variable annuities in Chapter 10). For variable annuity purchases, the customer does not pay the commission up front. Instead, the insurance company that issues the annuity pays the broker a commission immediately and recoups that money through annual fees that are deducted from the value of your investment. Variable annuities come with long surrender periods, during which withdrawals from the investment result in a surrender charge being deducted from the account. The surrender period, which can be as long as 10 years, is designed to make the investor hold the investment long enough for the insurance company to recoup the sales commission, plus some, through annual fees.

In the case of variable annuities, brokers are trained to respond to questions about commissions as follows: "You put a dollar into this investment, and the entire dollar goes to work for you." If you didn't know better, you might take that answer to mean that you won't have to pay a commission. But that is neither true nor, technically, what the broker said. The answer is evasive. While 100 percent of your money will be credited to your account, the insurance company will get the commission from you, either through exorbitant annual fees or through surrender charges. Lose any broker who evades the commission question with this tactic.

The vigilant investor asks about commissions and listens carefully to the initial response. You are listening for two things. First, does the broker answer the question that was asked? An honest response to the question would have to be phrased as a sum of money. If the initial answer does not end with the word *dollars*, the broker is avoiding the question. The broker knows what you want to know, but he is being evasive because he is afraid that you won't invest if you know the truth. That should tell you all you need to know about the investment and the broker.

The second thing that the vigilant investor listens for in the answer to the commission question is the substance of the answer. In the very unusual case in which the broker tells you the commission without first trying to avoid doing so, size up the answer. A commission of $15 on a stock trade will not have a material impact on the broker's production unless the broker is trading too often. A commission of $500, on the other hand, is big enough to blind an otherwise objective broker to the drawbacks of the investment. Certainly the enormous commission that a broker can earn on the sale of a single variable annuity should give you pause and lead you to take time to weigh the objectiveness of the advice. "What's in it for the broker?" is a fair question. The vigilant investor always gets the answer and carves out time to consider what it says about the broker's objectivity.

The Feedbag

Perhaps the most effective sales trick ever invented is the "free lunch" seminar. A brokerage firm finds a community of potential investors, usually of retirement age, and places ads in local newspapers announcing a supposed seminar on investing that will take place at a nice restaurant. Everyone who attends eats for free. "Space is limited," they say.

Investors flock to free lunch and free dinner seminars like teenage girls to a Justin Bieber concert. At the gathering, the brokerage firm presents the challenges of making your assets last in retirement, avoiding taxes, and/or making things easy for your heirs after you die. Having laid out the challenges, it gets down to the reason that it was willing to shell out hundreds of dollars to feed total strangers. The firm has the solution to those problems, the speaker says, and it wants you to buy the solution from it.

Different firms close the free lunch sale in different ways. Some want you to buy before you leave the restaurant. Others use the free lunch equivalent of the one-two punch and ask you to schedule a private meeting with a broker from the firm that sponsored the lunch. Often, that private meeting becomes another kind of meal at which the broker begins feeding off your life savings by selling you high-commission products like annuities or limited partnership investments.

There is nothing nefarious per se about buying a stranger a free meal, or about using the occasion to tell the stranger about your credentials and your business. But securities regulators have found that few such seminars follow FINRA, SEC, and state rules designed to protect investors. In 2007, the SEC published a report of the findings of a coordinated sweep of free lunch seminars. It teamed up with NASAA and FINRA to examine 110 such seminars. The regulators found that only 4 percent of the seminars were free from "problems or deficiencies." That's 4 percent. The vigilant investor doesn't like those odds and eats somewhere else.

Due Diligence for the Vigilant

The vigilant investor:

- Finds out where a broker learned how to sell and avoids those who learned it from a firm with a reputation for customer abuse
- Studies a broker's CRD for frequent job changes and avoids those who apparently can't follow the rules
- Objects to brokers' recommendations to gauge whether the broker is giving scripted responses
- Steers clear of any broker who uses high-pressure tactics like creating a sense of urgency
- Avoids a margin account if he is retired or nearing retirement
- Hangs up on a broker who tries the one-two punch
- Avoids any broker who won't disclose her commission immediately
- Considers the commission when assessing the broker's advice on an investment
- Knows that a "free lunch" might be the most expensive meal that an investor ever eats

10

Variable Annuities

Bells, Whistles, and Porcine Cosmetics

Variable annuities stink!

—CLARK HOWARD

I think variable annuities exist for one reason only: to make money for the financial advisers who sell them.

—SUZE ORMAN

In 2008, Marcus and Michelle Schrenker were living what seemed like the perfect Ken and Barbie lifestyle—a 10,000-square-foot home in an exclusive Indianapolis suburb, a 6,500-square-foot house in suburban Atlanta, luxury automobiles, boats, and airplanes. Having studied finance and aviation at Purdue University, Marcus Schrenker became an investment adviser and an accomplished stunt pilot. At 33 years old, he was already an impressive man. Everyone thought highly of him. More than 100 people had entrusted their financial future to him and his company, Heritage Wealth Management, Inc.

On January 10, 2009, Schrenker drove 500 miles from his home in Indiana to Harpersville in rural central Alabama, towing a red Yamaha street bike with saddlebags full of supplies. He rented a storage unit under an assumed name, parked the motorcycle there, and drove back home. The next evening, he took off from Anderson, Indiana, in a Piper Malibu airplane and headed south. When he could see the lights of Birmingham, Alabama, far off to the east, Schrenker sent out a distress call, claiming that the windshield of the aircraft had shattered and blown inward and that he was bleeding profusely. Air traffic controllers were not able to raise him on the radio after that, so they scrambled two Navy F-15s. The pilots found the plane flying on autopilot with the door open and the cabin lights out. The windshield was intact.

Schrenker had come to the end of his rope. That week, not only had he been served with a divorce complaint, but the Indiana Insurance Commission had filed charges against him for unauthorized and fraudulent sales of variable annuities. He had plenty of company; variable annuities have been the investment of choice for many avaricious brokers, because there is nothing they can sell you that will pay them a higher commission. In this chapter, we will examine what variable annuities are, why they are so attractive to brokers like Schrenker, and how the vigilant investor can accurately assess the risks and benefits of these investments.

Variable Annuity Basics

After his phony distress call, Schrenker put his plane on autopilot and parachuted out. The plane was on course for the Gulf of Mexico, where Schrenker expected the search for his body to last several days. *Sharks probably got him*, he hoped the Coast Guard would conclude. Instead, the plane, slowed by the drag from the open door, ran out of fuel and crashed just yards shy of a neighborhood of beachfront homes.

Schrenker floated down into a swampy area of rural Alabama. Being farther than he had expected from his intended drop zone, he knocked on the door of a house in Childersburg, Alabama, and asked for help. Local police responded and drove him to a motel in Harpersville, as Schrenker explained that he was wet from the knees down because he had been in a canoeing accident.

Schrenker checked into the motel but promptly set off on foot for the storage unit to retrieve the motorcycle. U.S. marshals found him on January 13, 2009, in a campground in Chattahoochee, Florida, moments after he had slashed his wrists. Only the marshals' quick work saved his life. In August 2009, a federal judge sentenced him to 51 months in prison on charges related to his phony distress call. In October 2010, he pleaded guilty to five state felony counts of securities fraud in connection with his variable annuity sales and theft from client accounts. The judge sentenced him to 10 years in prison, to be served after his federal time.

Notice that it was the Indiana *Insurance* Commission that pursued the investigation of Schrenker. Because variable annuities have a quasi-insurance component, insurance commissioners have jurisdiction to pursue fraudulent sales of these securities. The vigilant investor, therefore, asks state insurance commissioners, as well as securities commissioners, about any prospective annuity salesperson.

A variable annuity is a contract with an insurance company. You give the company your money, and the company agrees to give it back to you under certain conditions. You direct how the insurance company invests your money, choosing from several "subaccounts" that act like mutual funds inside the annuity. You can be conservative, putting all of your investment in a money market subaccount. You can be wildly speculative, putting all of your money in a small-cap stock subaccount. Or you can mix and match to suit your risk tolerance. If your subaccount choices perform well, the value of your account increases.

If your subaccount choices lose money, the value of your account drops. You do not pay taxes on any increase in the value of your account until you take money out.

An investment in a variable annuity usually ties up your money for between 6 and 10 years. The insurance company needs you to stay in the investment for that long so that it can take some of your money through annual fees. It uses those fees to recoup the large commission that it paid to the broker and to earn a healthy profit. If you withdraw your money during those years, the annuity company assesses a penalty, called a *surrender charge*, and takes that money out of your account. The bottom line is, once you buy a variable annuity, the insurance company *will* get its profit from you, either through the annual fees or through surrender charges.

Variable annuities also provide what is called a *death benefit*. It isn't really a benefit, because all your beneficiaries get back is the account value minus anything that you've taken out. That's no more than what they would receive under your will if you had invested in something else.

Some annuities allow you to buy additional death benefit features that keep the death benefit at the highest value the account reaches, even if it subsequently retreats from that high-water mark. They charge you extra for that benefit, of course. And they charge you enough to make sure that they come out ahead on the transaction.

You also have the option of letting the annuity company keep your investment and, in return, pay you a monthly benefit for the rest of your life. Opting for lifetime payments is called *annuitizing*. This erases any death benefit and converts the account value into that string of monthly payments; the insurance company decides how your monthly payment is calculated. According to recent statistics, 99 percent of people who buy an annuity do not annuitize.

The devil is in the details, and the details of any variable annuity are much more complicated than this overview suggests. The details of how the annuity works are included in a document called a *prospectus*. It's difficult reading, even for a lawyer. Most investors never read it, relying instead on the broker's verbal representations. But because the broker rarely reads or even understands the practically hieroglyphic language of the prospectus, he often says things in the sales pitch that are just not true. The insurance companies know this and protect themselves by including in the fine print of the prospectus a paragraph that says, essentially, "You cannot believe what the salesperson says, and we don't have to do what he or she promises you if it is inconsistent with the written details in this prospectus." In more than two decades of protecting investors, I've never met an investor who read that far into a prospectus.

The vigilant investor knows that the broker's representations are meaningless, and that a full understanding of what the annuity does and does not do requires a thorough, time-consuming analysis of the prospectus. Never buy an annuity, variable or otherwise, unless you've read every word of the prospectus. To be safe, get a lawyer to review the prospectus as well and explain the annuity's risks and benefits. What you hear from the lawyer will be drastically different from what you heard from the salesperson.

Brokers Fall Victim to Success: Annuity Flipping

In October 2005, prior to his arrest and conviction for securities fraud and making a phony distress call, Marcus Schrenker paid $1.65 million for his home in the exclusive Governor's Towne Club community in suburban Atlanta. From there, he had ready access to the retiring Delta

Air Lines pilots that he met at the air shows where he performed stunts. In the days before Delta's 2007 bankruptcy filing, Delta pilots in their fifties were retiring in droves and needed help deciding how to invest their retirement distributions. Schrenker had a plan: variable annuities. Several Delta pilots entrusted their nest eggs to Schrenker, and he made enormous commissions by selling them variable annuities.

But Schrenker, like most brokers who chase variable annuity commissions, had worked and spent himself into a corner. By locking his clients into variable annuities that carried surrender charges for as long as 10 years, he guaranteed that his clients would have no other money to invest for a decade. No money to invest means no more commissions. Schrenker's grandiose lifestyle quickly burned through the enormous commissions from the initial variable annuity sales. He found new clients, of course, but not enough to pay for his lifestyle. With all of his clients' investable assets tied up for as long as 10 years, Schrenker came to a moment of decision: He had to either drastically reduce his lifestyle so that he could live through a commission drought, or keep selling annuities at the same rate.

Schrenker (like many other brokers) decided to sell annuities to clients who already owned them, surrender penalties be damned. It happens so often that there is a name for it; it's called variable annuity *flipping*. It's the variable annuity equivalent of churning, which we discussed in Chapter 7.

Schrenker hid the large surrender charges from his clients by sending them phony account statements. Not every broker goes that far, or even needs to. As we'll discuss later in this chapter, the insurance companies understand the dilemma that their top producers face and have created products that help them convince holders of variable annuities to pay surrender charges in order to invest in another variable annuity.

Porcine Cosmetics

The outcry against variable annuities by consumer reporters and regulators has been so loud and so constant that insurance companies, like the prime bank scamsters we discussed in Chapter 3, have had to adapt and change. So they've come up with new "features" to address the many valid criticisms of variable annuities.

You may have heard the old expression "putting lipstick on a pig." Well, insurance companies and the brokers who sell annuities haven't stopped with lipstick in their effort to make variable annuities appear more attractive. They've thrown perfume and a Saks Fifth Avenue wardrobe on their pigs. As you might expect, the results are not glamorous; they're grotesque.

When regulators complained about sales of inherently illiquid variable annuities to senior citizens who might need access to the money before the surrender period ends, insurance companies began selling annuities that allow "free" withdrawals of up to 10 percent of the value of the account each year. But those withdrawal rights serve only to highlight the extreme restrictions on access to the money. Are we supposed to think that the insurance company is being generous for allowing us access to 10 percent of our money each year? Imagine a bank that markets its personal checking account with television ads announcing, "And at First National Bank, you can withdraw up to 10 percent of your balance each year!"

When regulators complained about variable annuity flipping, insurance companies began offering so-called bonuses for the purchase of new annuities. "We'll add 5 percent to the value of your account," they say. "That will more than cover the remaining 4 percent surrender charge you will have to pay to get out of your existing annuity." The vigilant investor will not be shocked to learn that the bonus is not really a bonus. You can't withdraw it until after the surrender period (if you can withdraw it at all), and the insurance company gets it back from you during that period by charging higher annual fees. Just how wise an investment could a variable annuity be if the company has to bribe you to buy it?

Free Lunch plus Variable Annuities Equals Indigestion

Between November 1999 and February 2007, four brokers from the brokerage firm Prime Capital Services, Inc., held a nonstop commission feast along the Atlantic Coast of Florida. The feast began with free lunch seminars in the towns of Melbourne, Boynton Beach, Delray Beach, and Boca Raton. Prime Capital gave the four brokers a free lunch script, and it worked to perfection. After the seminars, many attendees scheduled private meetings with one of Prime Capital's brokers. In June 2009, the SEC commenced an enforcement action against Prime Capital, its parent company, the four brokers, and their supervisors, alleging fraudulent sales of variable annuities and gross failure to supervise.

Eric J. Brown was a broker in Prime Capital's Delray Beach office. According to the SEC, in 2000 and 2001, he sold one elderly couple at least 10 variable annuities, earning commissions of $50,000 for Prime Capital and $20,000 for himself from these sales. After the sales, three-quarters of the couple's assets were tied up in illiquid variable annuities.

In 2000, according to the SEC, Brown convinced a 76-year-old widow to sell her diversified portfolio of stocks and bonds and invest 80 percent of the proceeds in variable annuities with surrender periods that would expire when she was in her early eighties. He earned $16,000 in commissions for himself and $16,000 for Prime Capital by doing so. But selling only a single variable annuity was not enough for Brown. Having sold the elderly widow one annuity, he soon convinced her to exchange it for another, earning himself another large commission, while costing her $20,000 in surrender fees.

In December 2003, after receiving complaints from Brown's customers, the State of Florida Department of Financial Services revoked Brown's license to sell insurance. He got his license back shortly thereafter by agreeing not to sell annuities to new customers over the age of 65.

Prime Capital did not fire Brown when he lost his license; he'd been making too much money for the firm. Instead, he continued selling variable annuities at free lunch seminars to people older than 65. According to the SEC, Brown's supervisor, Matthew J. Collins, helped Brown do so by signing the paperwork as if Collins had made the sales instead of Brown.

In 2004 and 2005, while Brown was prohibited from selling annuities to people over 65, he nevertheless convinced a couple in their eighties to exchange six annuities that they already owned for six new annuities. The elderly couple lost $61,000 in surrender charges. According to the SEC, branch manager Collins signed the paperwork as if he had made the sales.

Kevin J. Walsh was a broker in Prime Capital's office in Melbourne, Florida. According to the SEC, he flatly refused to submit his variable annuity sales to his supervisor for review. Walsh's supervisor notified Prime Capital's chief compliance officer of the refusal. The compliance officer notified Prime Capital's president. By now, you can guess what happened. Walsh sold hundreds of variable annuities while violating firm policies designed to protect customers. The chief compliance officer and the president of the brokerage firm knew about it but took no action to stop him. During 2004, Walsh earned $385,000 in variable annuity commissions for Prime Capital, and the same amount for himself.

Mark W. Wells was a broker in Prime Capital's Boca Raton office. In 2006, he convinced an 80-year-old widow to exchange a variable annuity from which she could have withdrawn money without a surrender charge for a new annuity with a six-year surrender period. Half of the widow's net worth was tied up in the annuity. Wells earned a $6,000 commission on the sale. In 2004 and 2005, he convinced a 65-year-old retired man to buy six variable annuities with eight-year surrender periods. Those purchases locked up two-thirds of the man's savings in the variable annuities. Wells earned approximately $16,000 in commissions for himself.

In 2010, the SEC ordered Prime Capital to cease and desist from violation of the antifraud provisions of the federal securities laws. It fined Prime Capital's parent company $450,000 and ordered Prime Capital to pay disgorgement totaling $144,262 to its victims. The SEC barred Brown, Collins, Walsh, and Wells from working in the securities industry and ordered each to pay disgorgement and a $130,000 civil penalty.

Brokers Being Sold

Brokers learn what little they know about variable annuities from people called *wholesalers*. The wholesaler is either an employee of the insurance company or an independent contractor who gets a cut of every annuity sold. It is her job to convince a broker that the newest annuity from the wholesaler's company is perfect for every single customer.

Wholesalers spend more time in brokerage offices than you ever will. Like the middleman who supplies refrigerators to Home Depot, the wholesaler establishes a good relationship with every branch manager in her territory and calls often. When there's a new annuity to sell, the wholesaler calls the branch manager of a local office and offers to buy the whole office lunch if she can show the employees a PowerPoint presentation about the new variable annuity. The branch manager says yes, and the wholesaler makes the presentation, which sets forth certain features of the annuity: the bonuses, the withdrawal rights, and so on.

Usually the wholesaler saves the best for last. Even brokers who have been dozing through the presentation perk up when they are told that the insurance company is paying an extra percentage point in commission to anyone who sells this annuity in the next 90 days. This incentive always has the desired effect. Every broker in the room is at least tempted to sell as many of those annuities as possible while the higher commission is still available. If the brokers think about their customers' objectives at all, they will rationalize: "Maybe the annuity will perform very well, and the customer will be happy." That might happen. Then again, in a world in which anything is possible, Boston might give Derek Jeter the key to the city. Back in the real world, the broker knows that, whatever happens to you, he will earn thousands of dollars on the sale.

In my law practice, I routinely get documents called *commission runs* that show what the broker was selling and how much commission he earned. In a variable annuity case, I always see the same pattern. I see several purchases of a particular company's annuity, let's say Hartford, for a period of two to four weeks. Then sales of the Hartford annuities stop abruptly, and there are several sales of Pacific Life annuities and only Pacific Life annuities. Soon Pacific Life disappears from the commission run and Prudential takes its place. The explanation for that pattern is that the broker was selling whichever annuity paid the biggest commission at the time. When the limited-time-only commission offer on the Hartford annuities expired, the broker looked for the next "extra point" opportunity and began selling that.

Wholesalers also offer sales tips that are specific to the annuity they are promoting. Like Olde Discount, they tell brokers how to handle common objections to buying the annuity. Beyond the tips offered by wholesalers, though, brokers can earn the sales equivalent of a Ph.D. in annuity sales by attending classes that teach sales techniques. At those classes, salespeople learn to talk to senior citizens as if they are talking to 12-year-olds and to scare investors about the safety of their money in FDIC-insured bank accounts by saying that the FDIC is insolvent and takes years to pay the claims of depositors at failed banks. In fact, while the FDIC keeps only enough cash on hand to cover expected failures, it has never failed to make insured depositors whole, and it pays claims in a matter of days, not years. Contrary to the suggestion that annuities are safer than FDIC-insured deposits, annuities are eggs-in-one-basket bets on the solvency of the insurance company that issues them. That may not have seemed like much of a gamble until September 2008, when insurance giant AIG—once the eighteenth largest public company in the world—needed a government bailout to avoid insolvency.

The Shortest Distance Between Two Points

There are ethical brokers out there, brokers who understand that the name of the game is production, but who shoot for a long-term career—rather than quick riches—by letting their customers' best interest determine their commissions rather than letting commissions cloud their perception of what is in the customer's best interest. I met one of them when I coached his son in baseball.

Tom was the father of my center fielder. He was a stockbroker at a bank-based brokerage firm. After practice one day, he asked my advice. He told me that most of his clients were nearing retirement and held a mix of high-grade municipal bonds and dividend-paying stocks. Like all brokers, Tom had a production target that he had to meet or exceed each year. He told me that he had gotten a new branch manager in the middle of the year and that the new branch manager had doubled his production target for the remainder of the year. "Pat," Tom said, "I cannot possibly make that number unless I sell my clients' bonds and conservative stocks and buy them all variable annuities." I referred Tom to an employment lawyer, and I was not surprised when he changed firms rather than sell out his clients to meet his new production goals.

Firms set their brokers' production targets high. The rewards for meeting or exceeding them are substantial. The punishment for failure is unemployment. Often those targets come with the implicit statement from the firm: "We're not saying that you have to sell annuities, but we all know that meeting your production goal without doing so will be next to impossible." If the broker works for an independent firm and therefore is responsible for her own costs of doing business (rent, payroll, utilities, and so on), selling variable annuities is the quickest way to cover her overhead and to prosper. The broker who shuns the variable annuity road to quick riches is the exception.

The Congenitally Honest Variable Annuity Salesman

I like to daydream about a variable annuity salesman with a congenital condition that compels him to tell the whole truth about what he is selling without any attempts at salesmanship. No half-truths. No attempts to conceal. Just the unvarnished truth as best he can tell it, followed by scrupulously honest answers to every question. His best friends are Santa and Sasquatch, of course. Here's his side of a variable annuity pitch:

> Here's the deal. You give us your life savings, and we'll put it in an account with your name on it. If you need it back this year, we'll give you 90 percent of the balance of the account and keep 10 percent for ourselves. If you need it back in five years, we'll give you back 95 percent of the balance of the account and keep only 5 percent. If you leave it with us for 10 years, though, we'll give you back the entire balance of the account!
>
> What's in it for us? Do you mean for me or for the insurance company? For me, it's a $7,000 commission. For the insurance company, it's 3 percent per year, which adds up to about 30 percent deducted from the account over the 10-year surrender period.
>
> Not interested? Did I mention that you can invest the account any way you like? You can invest in 20 different stock funds and 20 different bond funds.
>
> Pardon? Well, if those funds lose money, then the balance of the account would decline by that amount. If the funds increase in value, the balance of the account goes up by that amount.
>
> Come again? Well, I guess that follows. Given the 30 percent that the annuity company is taking, the funds would have to increase by more than 30 percent over the 10 years before you would make the first cent of profit.
>
> Please, please, don't say no before I get the rest of the facts out. There is also a death benefit payable to your beneficiary if you die. The amount? I was hoping you would ask that. If you die, your beneficiary gets 100 percent of the account value or the amount of your deposits into the account, whichever is greater, minus anything

that you have taken out of the account. No, he doesn't get anything else. Yes, I guess he would get that money anyway under your will if you bought a different investment.

Wait, wait, wait, don't leave. I was saving the best part for last. We will deposit an additional 4 percent into the account if you buy now. Well, no, you cannot withdraw that 4 percent. You will not get that unless you leave your money in the account for 10 years, and the annual fee is higher, so that the annuity company can make back that 4 percent.

My what? My honest opinion? I wouldn't buy one of these, but I really want the commission that the insurance company is going to pay me if you buy one. So, what do you say?

That is an honest variable annuity pitch. Why do so many baby boomers nearing retirement own them, then? Two reasons: first, because the leading wave of baby boomers has decades' worth of savings with which to buy big ones, and second, because brokers are trained in how to sell them. Can you trust a broker who would pitch you a variable annuity without disclosing any of the things our congenitally honest broker disclosed? The vigilant investor does not.

Einstein on Variable Annuities

Einstein taught us that time and space are relative. He could have said the same thing about the benefits of variable annuities. Compared to throwing your money into a hole in the ground where water and worms will eat away 4 percent of the money every year, a variable annuity that eats up only 3 percent of your money every year in annual fees—and might actually grow—sounds pretty good until you consider that if you want to get your money out of the hole in the ground, you can dig it up anytime and keep 100 percent of whatever is there. You can't do that with a variable annuity. Your money has to stay there until the annuity company has eaten up 20 to 30 percent of it in annual fees. Then you can get it back. To have any hope of earning more than the cost of the annuity, you will have to allocate a substantial amount of your investment to riskier subaccounts; the most conservative allocation will not generate a return that even keeps pace with the annual fees.

So we have to think hard to come up with a worse alternative than a variable annuity. And I've thought of one. As a place to keep your hard-earned savings, a variable annuity wins hands down over an incinerator. A vigilant investor knows that any investment that, by its terms, intends to take 30 percent of your principal over 10 years is a poor alternative to a hole in the ground.

Insurance companies must change their act occasionally to keep things fresh. Many brokers have fled the bad press about variable annuities and have begun selling products called equity-indexed annuities instead. While they are not variable annuities, equity-indexed annuities suffer from the same deficiencies: long surrender periods and objectivity-shattering commissions for the salesperson. Whatever label a broker gives you for an investment issued by an insurance company, investigate the surrender period, the commission that the broker is earning, and the annual cost of owning the investment.

Due Diligence for the Vigilant

The vigilant investor:

► Reads every word of the annuity prospectus (getting help with understanding it, if necessary) before buying an annuity

➤ Investigates an annuity salesperson through state insurance commissioners, as well as through securities regulators

➤ Values a broker who has never tried to sell him a high-commission investment

➤ Rejects any investment that penalizes her for accessing her money

➤ Realizes that the most conservative investment inside a variable annuity will not keep pace with the annual fees and will therefore result in a guaranteed loss

➤ Never buys an investment offered by an insurance company without assessing the surrender charges, the cost of owning the investment, and the salesperson's commission

11

Making Sense of Alphabet Soup

RIAs, CFAs, CFPs, and Your Friendly
Neighborhood Insurance Agent

It is not titles that honor men, but men that honor titles.

—Niccolò Machiavelli

As the president of SEC-registered investment adviser F&S Asset Management Group in Jacksonville, Florida, Wayne McLeod carved out a profitable niche as a consultant to federal law enforcement officers. He conducted seminars for FBI special agents, DEA agents, and Customs and Border Patrol officers. McLeod helped the attendees understand the benefits to which they were entitled and advised them on how to allocate their retirement accounts. But he also offered something more to those who had extra cash to invest: a government bond fund paying between 8 and 10 percent per year. More than 250 agents put their savings into the bond fund.

The fund never existed. McLeod used the $34 million he collected to maintain a luxurious lifestyle: condominiums on exclusive Amelia Island; a skybox at EverBank Field, where the NFL's Jacksonville Jaguars play; annual trips to the Super Bowl; luxury cars; a riverfront mansion; and a 38-foot boat, on which he regularly entertained his clients. McLeod also used some of the money to sponsor golf tournaments for the DEA Survivors Benefit Fund and to make distributions to earlier investors to maintain the façade of legitimacy. On June 22, 2010, having admitted his crimes to the SEC after two days of questioning, McLeod drove his black Hummer to Mandarin Park on the banks of the St. Johns River, put a handgun to his right temple, and committed suicide.

Very little of what McLeod had told his clients was true. But he was indeed an SEC-registered investment adviser (RIA). In this chapter, we will find out what RIAs are, what they are not, and how the Dodd-Frank Act of 2010 might make it more difficult for investors to choose between a broker and an RIA. We'll also look at some of the securities industry designations that RIAs and brokers earn (such as CFP and CFA) to set themselves apart from the crowd and take a look at how insurance agents (with their own designations) have entered the investment business. Finally, we will show vigilant investors how to steer their nest eggs safely through the maze of titles and industry designations.

Registered Investment Advisers

Wayne McLeod made sure that his law enforcement clients knew that he was an RIA, a different animal entirely from the stockbrokers we've been discussing thus far. RIAs owe a higher duty to their clients—a fiduciary duty. Unlike stockbrokers, RIAs are registered with the SEC or a state's securities agency and must put their clients' interests first and disclose all potential conflicts of interest.

Perhaps the best way to illustrate the impact of an RIA's fiduciary duty is to consider the sale of a variable annuity that will pay the salesperson a $10,000 commission. A stockbroker is allowed to make a pitch for this investment without ever mentioning how that prospective windfall creates a conflict between the broker's financial interest and the customer's interest. An RIA is bound by his fiduciary duty to disclose the commission (even if the client does not ask), to identify it as a potential conflict, and to act in the client's best interest.

Because of their fiduciary duty, most RIAs do not accept commissions. Instead, many charge their clients a fee—typically between 1 and 2 percent of the value of the account annually. Ideally, that compensation structure aligns the RIA's interests with her clients' interests. Other RIAs instead charge an hourly rate for their services. Still others charge a flat fee for producing a comprehensive financial plan. The vigilant investor asks prospective RIAs how they get paid and what services they provide in return for that compensation.

Most RIAs will have you open a brokerage account at a discount brokerage firm (such as Charles Schwab or Fidelity Investments) and execute paperwork that gives the RIA authority to make trades in your account. When you put your assets under the control of the RIA, you write the check to the brokerage firm, not the RIA. There is a measure of safety in that arrangement, since you will receive monthly statements from the brokerage firm that you can compare against the statements that you receive from the RIA. Because the independent brokerage firm maintains physical custody of your assets, it is more difficult for a dishonest RIA to remove assets from your account.

A few RIAs are registered as both RIAs and stockbrokers. Those with dual registration can receive commissions (as the stockbroker) on any trades they place (as the RIA) in your account. Just as troubling as the inevitable temptation to generate commissions is the fact that your assets are in the custody of the RIA's brokerage firm. In that situation, there is no truly independent brokerage firm keeping watch over your account, which is why you should ask any prospective RIA whether she is dually registered and who will maintain custody of your assets. Keep in mind that it is always safer to have an independent firm holding your nest egg.

The distinction between RIAs and stockbrokers is supposed to be similar to that between medical doctors and pharmacists. Ideally, the doctor (RIA) diagnoses the ailment and prescribes medicine to treat it, and the pharmacist (stockbroker) fills the prescription. But by making use of an exemption in the Investment Advisers Act of 1940, brokers have encroached on the RIAs' territory so far and so often—both providing the diagnosis *and* filling prescriptions—that the distinction between the two has been lost on the investing public. Dually registered RIAs blur the lines further. When is this individual wearing his "RIA hat," and when is he wearing his "stockbroker hat"? A 2008 RAND Corporation study commissioned by the SEC found that the vast majority of investors don't know the difference between RIAs and brokers and, mistakenly, believe that both are required to act in the investor's best interests.[1] The vigilant investor knows better.

"SEC Approved"

James Freese made sure everyone knew that he was not a stockbroker. He was quick to tell prospective clients about the fiduciary duties he owed as an RIA and to reassure them that an independent brokerage firm would maintain custody of their assets. If only he had lived up to those representations.

Freese opened his investment advisory firm, AFG Capital Management, Inc., in Overland Park, Kansas, in 2002. He told the more than 100 people who gave him their nest eggs that he was opening accounts for them at Charles Schwab and that he would make their accounts grow through traditional securities trading in stocks, bonds, and mutual funds. In all, Freese managed $8 million.[2] The clients received monthly statements from Freese that included their Charles Schwab account numbers, but they received no separate statements from Charles Schwab.

Freese appeared to be success incarnate, and it comforted his clients to see him so prosperous: *If the man who manages my money is doing that well, imagine how well my investments must be faring.* Their monthly statements from AFG confirmed it. Their account balances grew impressively, and their monthly distribution checks arrived right on time.

Things began to unravel for Freese when one of his clients stopped by a local Charles Schwab office to check on the balance of his account. Schwab said that it had no such account. The Kansas Securities Commissioner sent an audit team to AFG's offices. What the team members found there gave them more than enough evidence to revoke Freese's investment advisory registration and refer the case to the Johnson County, Kansas, district attorney's office.

Freese had been running a classic Ponzi scheme. He had never opened brokerage accounts for his clients. He had never ordered a single securities trade. He had simply deposited the checks, which his clients had made payable to AFG, and used the money to make phony distribution payments to early marks and to support his lifestyle.

In August 2007, Freese pleaded guilty to one count of securities fraud for defrauding his church of $513,800, three counts of investment adviser fraud for defrauding 116 advisory clients of more than $6.2 million, and five counts of making false writings through phony account statements. In October 2007, the judge sentenced him to seven years in prison. With good behavior, he will be out in five. He will be only 41 years old.

Freese was not the first scam artist to tout his status as an RIA, nor will he be the last. The fiduciary duty that comes with that status has always been a major selling point for RIAs. But becoming an RIA requires little more than filling out the appropriate paperwork. There are no minimum education requirements, and the examination that some states require of RIA representatives (the Series 65 examination) is not especially challenging. Neither the SEC nor any other regulator certifies that RIAs are good at what they do. Since regulators are understaffed and underfunded, many RIAs go five years or more between regulatory examinations, more than enough time to run a Ponzi scheme. Yet some RIAs lead prospective clients to believe that registration represents a regulatory thumbs-up on their business practices. It doesn't.

The vigilant investor knows that a legitimate RIA, as often as she might correctly point out her fiduciary duty, will never imply that registration provides a regulatory seal of approval. Any RIA who suggests that it does is angling to steal your nest egg. Avoid such RIAs at all costs, and do your fellow investors a favor—call the SEC. The SEC's examination staff would love to pay that investment adviser a surprise visit.

It pays to understand the fiduciary duties that RIAs owe, but never take it on faith that your RIA is living up to those duties. Had one of Freese's clients sought to confirm the existence of his supposed

Schwab account earlier, Freese's career as a scam artist might have been much shorter and the number of scrambled nest eggs fewer. Insist on statements from the brokerage firm that holds your assets, and compare those statements to the statements you receive from your RIA.

RIA as Hedge Fund Manager

Chester County, Pennsylvania, lies one hour west of Philadelphia. It is known as horse country. Very smart, very wealthy people from Chester County commute to Philadelphia and return at night to homes on acreage with enough land for barns, paddocks, pastures, and jump rings. At cocktail parties, they talk about the lineage of their horses and the races in which they are entered for the coming season.

Donald Anthony Walker ("Tony") Young was a regular on the Chester County cocktail circuit, where he spoke about his own horses and his latest commute, via limousine and private jet, to his $2.1 million vacation home in Palm Beach, Florida. In those conversations, the talk inevitably involved a back-and-forth about respective occupations. "I'm a registered investment adviser and a hedge fund manager," Young would say. When people asked him how his hedge funds were performing, he would give glowing reports on how much money his investors were making.

Inevitably, some of those cocktail conversations led to lunches at the Coatesville Country Club, where Young would give more details about his Acorn II L.P. hedge fund. Anxious to earn enough to mate their filly with a first-class stud, more than 40 of Young's Chester County neighbors entrusted him with more than $23 million.

It was all a lie. In April 2010, a federal grand jury indicted Young on one count of mail fraud and one count of money laundering arising from his Ponzi scheme. In July 2010, Young pleaded guilty to both counts. As of this writing, he is still awaiting sentencing.

The vigilant investor pays attention to whether an RIA is also managing a hedge fund or some other investment pool. An RIA who solicits clients to invest in a hedge fund that he manages cannot be objective about the wisdom of investing in that fund. If your RIA solicits you to invest in a fund that he manages, explain that you will need two things first: an independent due diligence report on the fund and the name of an objective RIA who can advise you about the wisdom of investing in that fund. If the RIA refuses either request, avoid the fund and find another RIA.

What Hath Dodd-Frank Wrought?

The Dodd-Frank Act was a sweeping attempt at giving investors more protection—tighter regulation of hedge funds, money for hiring more examiners to audit RIAs more often, and funding to allow regulators to keep up with the technological advances in the market. Whether the reforms mandated by that act will ever come to pass will depend upon whether the new Congress will appropriate enough money to allow them to proceed. Unfortunately, that answer will be driven by political, rather than investor protection, motives. The securities industry is very well funded and has a financial interest in business as usual. Fortunately, the vigilant investor has the tools to navigate the investing landscape in any regulatory environment.

The Dodd-Frank Act gave the SEC the authority to harmonize the duties owed by stockbrokers and RIAs, but it did not mandate that change. Many commentators expect the SEC to give stockbrokers a fiduciary duty equal to the duty that RIAs have had all along. If it does so, the transition is bound to be rocky for stockbrokers, who are accustomed to being salespeople rather than fiduciaries. Whether "old dog" brokers, who are hardwired to pitch stocks and variable annuities to maximize their commissions, are even capable of adhering to "new trick" fiduciary standards is doubtful. If the SEC insists on the change, the transition might last a generation and require a complete revamping of how new brokers are trained.

As a business proposition, brokerage firms cannot abide a fiduciary standard. These firms maximize their profits through strict production quotas and intensive sales training for their brokers. A standard that requires brokers to put the interests of investors before the firm's bottom line would drastically reduce a firm's revenue. If the SEC saddles the brokerage industry with that standard, investors can expect the industry to push back against it with every lobbying dollar it can muster.

Faced with a fiduciary standard that it cannot measure up to, the brokerage industry would probably work by degrees to shorten the measuring stick, pushing for regulatory rules that would allow the industry to continue with something close to business as usual while declaring that it meets the new fiduciary standard. Firms might meet their fiduciary duty to disclose all potential conflicts of interest by "disclosing" them in densely worded prospectuses or account-opening documentation. But the RAND study revealed that most investors do not read written disclosures. Therefore, if the SEC allows brokerage firms to comply with their heightened duties through additional written disclosures alone, those heightened duties will provide little additional protection for investors.

Alternatively, the SEC might choose to increase the standards for stockbrokers, but to leave those standards just short of the fiduciary requirements that RIAs must meet. Such an approach would at least allow vigilant investors a clear choice between fiduciaries and nonfiduciaries. Whatever the SEC does with the standards of care for brokers and RIAs, however, investors will have to remain vigilant or risk having their nest eggs damaged in an environment in which the standards are unclear.

In an environment of shifting duties and poorly understood titles, RIAs and brokers are desperate to distinguish themselves from the crowd that is competing for control of the approximately $20 trillion in assets held by baby boomers and senior citizens. Many of them try to set themselves apart by earning "designations"—certification that they have completed an advanced course of study and/or passed an examination indicating their mastery of the subject matter.

CFAs and CFPs

Perhaps the most difficult industry designation to earn is the Chartered Financial Analyst (CFA) designation, issued by the CFA Institute. The CFA is recognized the world over. Those who aspire to be CFA charterholders engage in a graduate-level self-study course covering different types of securities, complex asset vehicles, quantitative analysis, and assessment of the relative value and risk of investments. Aspiring CFAs must pass three separate examinations. The historical pass rates for those examinations speak to their difficulty. For the 2010 examination cycle, only 42 percent passed the Level I examination, 39 percent passed the Level II examination, and 46 percent passed the Level III examination. Successful CFA candidates must also have 48 months of qualified professional work experience. There are approximately 90,000 CFA charterholders worldwide.

While it is not as difficult to earn as the CFA designation, the Certified Financial Planner (CFP®) designation, awarded by the Certified Financial Planner Board of Standards Inc., requires intensive study and passage of a challenging examination. It requires mastery of roughly 100 areas spanning the subjects of economics, finance, taxation, insurance, pensions and benefits, estate planning, and retirement planning. The CFP examination lasts 10 hours over a day and a half. In the decade between 2001 and 2010, pass rates for the CFP exam ranged from a high of 63 percent in November 2004 to a low of 50 percent in July 2009. It's no gimme. As of this writing, approximately 62,000 people hold CFP certification. The CFP board also has a disciplinary arm that investigates allegations of misconduct against CFP certificants and imposes sanctions up to and including revocation of the certificate.

CFPs and CFAs know much more about finance than how to pitch a stock and what happens to bond prices when interest rates rise. Vigilant investors can safely rely on those designations as indicators of mastery of the subject matter. But no vigilant investor allows an industry designation, no matter how hard it is to earn, to substitute for a thorough due diligence investigation. Accepting a designation as a shortcut for due diligence often leads to financial ruin.

James F. Putman of Appleton, Wisconsin, was a CFP certificant. In July 2002, *Worth* magazine named him one of the "Top 250 Financial Advisors in America." The November 2006 issue of *Medical Economics* magazine included Putman among the "Top 150 Best Advisors for Doctors." From 1996 to 1997, he served as president of the National Association of Personal Financial Advisors (NAPFA), a group that seeks to "provide independent financial advice that's not clouded by compensation based on the purchase or sale of a financial product"; you won't find a NAPFA member pushing annuities.

Putman was the founder and majority owner of SEC-registered investment adviser Wealth Management LLC. Most of his clients were wealthy individuals. According to the SEC, in 2006 and 2007, Putman and Wealth Management's former president and chief investment officer, Simone Fevola, breached their fiduciary duty to clients by accepting $1.24 million in undisclosed payments from unregistered investment pools in exchange for directing Wealth Management clients into those pools. In March 2010, Fevola settled the charges without admitting or denying the SEC's allegations. As of this writing, Putman is awaiting trial.

Additional Designations

Beyond the CFA and the CFP lies a jungle of additional designations, each of which suggests a level of advanced competence. A 2010 *Wall Street Journal* article by Jason Zweig and Mary Pilon, entitled "Is Your Advisor Pumping Up His Credentials?" addressed the confusing array of designations. Zweig and Pilon's research revealed more than 200 separate industry designations, some available for as little as a weekend of study and passage of a 100-question multiple-choice test. All of the designations sound impressive—Certified Senior Adviser, Chartered Senior Financial Planner, Certified Senior Specialist, Certified Retirement Financial Advisor—and that is the point. Brokers and RIAs alike want to be able to pitch themselves as experts. Some of the acronyms for these designations, like the Chartered Senior Financial Planner (CSFP) designation, look similar to designations that are extremely hard to earn (CFP). A not-yet-vigilant investor might mistakenly believe that the organization that awards the CSFP is affiliated with the CFP Board of Standards, or that the organization that awards the Certified Retirement Financial Advisor (CRFA) designation is affiliated with the CFA Institute. They aren't.

While the courses of study for some of these designations impart valuable information, the designations might imply more than they should to the not-yet-vigilant investor. How much safer is your money with an adviser because she has attended a weekend seminar and received a certificate at the end? For some of the additional designations that RIAs and brokers boast, a quote from Groucho Marx is apropos: "I don't want to belong to any club that will accept me as a member."

The vigilant investor gives no credit to a designation until he understands what it means. Begin your investigation of someone who claims to have an industry designation by finding out whether he actually has it. You can search for CFP certificants at www.cfp.net/search and search for disciplinary actions against CFPs at www.cfp.net/Learn/disciplineactions.asp. You can also confirm CFA representations on the "Investor Education" section of the CFA Institute's web site, www.cfainstitute.org. If a prospective investment adviser claims a designation that you are unfamiliar with, ask her what is required to earn that designation. Ask whether passing a test is required, and then ask what percentage of the people who take the test pass it. Finally, confirm those answers via an Internet search, and with a call to the organization that issued the designation if the information is not available on the Web.

Whom Can I Trust?

The 2008 RAND study found that investors choose their financial advisers primarily by asking one question: *Whom can I trust?* The vigilant investor asks the same question but considers it in two parts. Part 1 is, *Whom can I trust to have the knowledge and experience to give me sound advice?* Part 2 is, *Whom can I trust not to lie to me/withhold important information from me/steal my nest egg?*

The vigilant investor knows that impressive industry designations are reliable indicators for answering Part 1 of the trust question, but of very little use for answering Part 2. Unfortunately, while designations can tell us something about a person's diligence, his ambition, and his intelligence, they cannot tell us anything at all about how he will respond to the pressure that mounts when he has not earned enough fees and the mortgage is past due.

While the fiduciary duties that RIAs owe are a plus for investors who need guidance, you have to look far beyond those duties, answering Part 2 of the trust question with a vigilant due diligence investigation. Confirming registered status through the SEC at www.adviserinfo.sec.gov or through state regulators is the first step. Check the page of the adviser's Form ADV that lists the states in which the adviser is authorized to do business. If your state is not on the list, stay away. PACER will allow you to check for bankruptcies, federal convictions, and lawsuits filed in federal court. Be sure to search not only for the adviser's name, but also for all business names you know about. Confirm educational credentials through the National Student Clearinghouse, check for aliases and judgments through LexisNexis, and search for state lawsuits at the court clerk's office.

Your Friendly Neighborhood Insurance Agent

While most investors rely on RIAs or stockbrokers for financial advice, the insurance lobby has made certain that the SEC does not have jurisdiction over insurance agents who sell investments. Instead, state securities commissioners regulate insurance agents. That lack of federal oversight has allowed insurance agents to enter the investment playing field, selling annuities to investors who do not realize that the federal investment cops do not walk that beat. Without understanding the limits of what insurance agents are allowed to sell (only investments offered by an insurance company), many investors have mistakenly begun to accept insurance agents as legitimate salespeople for all types of investments. Making things even more difficult for investors, many insurance companies have created brokerage firm or investment advisory affiliates and registered their insurance agents as representatives of those entities, thereby allowing them to sell investments other than annuities.

Insurance agent Robert Sturman was a Little League coach in Bucks County, Pennsylvania. He had moved to the town of Feasterville Trevose (population 6,500) in the mid-1980s, and he had a good reputation. Many of his clients were current and retired public school teachers in Philadelphia. As far as anyone knew, he was still registered as an agent for Lincoln National Life Insurance Company in 2000 when he opened a new company called Retirement Planning Associates, Inc. Little did anyone know that Lincoln National had fired Sturman in 1999 for not selling enough annuities.

In 2000, Sturman began offering his clients investments in what he described as "fixed-return investments," paying supposed profits of 7 percent. He also convinced several clients that he could make large profits for them by buying blocks of tickets to sporting events and concerts and selling them at a profit. For a while, everyone was pleased with the returns that Sturman delivered on those investments. Among the clients who trusted him was Fredric Weiss. A retired Philadelphia science teacher, Weiss was dying of cancer when he asked Sturman to make sure that his wife, Cynthia, would have a secure financial future. "Everything will be fine," Sturman told him. Less than two years later, Sturman had stolen $600,000 from Mrs. Weiss and more than $3.6 million from 50 of his other clients, spending much of it at casinos in Atlantic City.

In July 2010, Sturman pleaded guilty to 15 counts of mail fraud, wire fraud, and interstate transportation of stolen property. He confessed to a gambling addiction at his sentencing hearing and suggested that his ex-wife's spending habits were at least partially responsible for his crimes. Sentenced to 10 years, he is awaiting assignment to a federal prison.

The vigilant investor uses the same resources she uses to perform due diligence on a broker or an RIA to seek information about an insurance agent. Search for federal lawsuits, criminal history, and bankruptcies through PACER, state lawsuits through a state courthouse records search, civil judgments and aliases through LexisNexis, and education through the National Student Clearinghouse. If the insurance agent is also registered with the brokerage firm subsidiary of his life insurance company, your state securities commissioner will be able to produce a CRD report on him.

Like RIAs and stockbrokers, insurance agents are in a crowded and highly competitive business. And, like RIAs and stockbrokers, they seek industry designations to burnish their résumés. Among the most sought-after insurance designations are the Chartered Life Underwriter (CLU) and the Chartered Financial Consultant (ChFC). Both require a course of study. But neither requires a test as demanding as those that CFAs and CFPs must pass.

Remember that an investment is an investment, regardless of whom the salesperson works for. Insurance agents do not owe fiduciary duties. While their long record of doing business in your town, their service as a Little League coach, and their obvious charisma might project an image of eminent trustworthiness, insurance agents, like stockbrokers, are salespeople who are seeking to maximize their commissions.

Due Diligence for the Vigilant

The vigilant investor:

▶ Asks prospective RIAs how they get paid and what they do for that compensation

▶ Insists that any assets managed by an RIA are located at an independent brokerage firm

▶ Knows that a legitimate RIA will never imply that registration provides a regulatory seal of approval

▶ Understands the fiduciary duties that RIAs owe, but never takes it on faith that his RIA is living up to those duties

▶ Insists on an independent due diligence report and advice from an unbiased RIA if the RIA recommends the purchase of a fund that she manages

▶ Gives no credit to an industry designation until he understands what it means, and never accepts it as a substitute for a full due diligence investigation

▶ Remembers that an investment is an investment, regardless of whom the salesperson works for, and uses the same resources that she uses to perform due diligence on a broker or an RIA to seek information about insurance agents

12

Low-Hanging Fruit

Seniors, the Sick, and the Solution

Honor your father and your mother.

—Exodus 20:12

Never doubt that a small group of thoughtful, committed citizens can change the world. Indeed, it is the only thing that ever has.

—Margaret Mead

Josephine Fergo was born in New York in 1906. She left high school after the ninth grade, at the age of 15. In 1926, when Babe Ruth strode the streets of Manhattan, Josephine took an administrative job at Bloomingdale's, where she worked for the next 69 years before retiring in 1995, at the age of 89. By that time, her pension account was worth $648,000, and she had other assets that she and her late husband had saved.

Four years before she retired, Josephine hired stockbroker and

RIA Mary Dietrick of PSA Equities, Inc. (PSA). What happened in the years that followed underscores the danger that faces every investor who lives to reach retirement. In this chapter, we will examine stockbroker abuse of senior citizens. We will also provide tools—including a template for a conversation with elderly parents—that vigilant investors can use to protect family members and friends who would otherwise be easy prey for unethical brokers. Finally, we ask vigilant investors to band together and reshape the investing landscape as no Congress or regulator can.

Abuse of the Most Vulnerable

Mary Dietrick insinuated herself into Josephine's life and finances in 1991, when she convinced Josephine to buy an annuity issued by Western Reserve Life Insurance Company. Although Josephine made her nephew, Carl Fergo, beneficiary of the annuity, shortly thereafter, Dietrick was named beneficiary. The request for the change came in a handwritten letter from Dietrick supposedly signed by Josephine.

The exploitation continued and accelerated. In 1993, Josephine made Dietrick the beneficiary on an annuity issued by Unity Mutual Life Insurance Company. Dietrick soon changed the address of record for that annuity from Josephine's address to her own. Josephine never received another piece of mail from Unity Mutual. In 1995, Dietrick had Josephine roll the Unity Mutual annuity into one issued by Principal Mutual Life Insurance Company, which Dietrick had chosen because it was one of only a few companies that would issue an annuity to someone as old as Josephine. Dietrick and her husband were named as the beneficiaries; their home address was the address of record.

In 1994, Dietrick obtained a written power of attorney over Josephine's financial affairs. When Josephine retired in 1995, Dietrich had her entire $648,000 pension balance paid out in a taxable distribution and deposited into a PSA brokerage account that she controlled rather than having it rolled into an IRA account, which would have avoided any tax consequences. The transaction subsequently created a $100,000 tax liability for Josephine.

Dietrick quickly began using the funds in the PSA account for her own benefit, transferring $130,000 from Josephine's PSA account into a new joint account with Josephine and Dietrick as co-owners. Before Josephine died, Dietrick transferred all of the securities in the joint account into a new PSA account in her name alone.

In 1997, Dietrick took Josephine to an attorney, who created a trust for the distribution of Josephine's assets; Dietrick was named as trustee and one of the beneficiaries. A year later, she took Josephine to the Atlantic Liberty Savings Bank in New York and had her transfer $50,000 into a new joint account. When Josephine's death appeared imminent, Dietrick withdrew all the money.

When Josephine died in December 1998, Dietrick collected $77,000 from the Western Reserve Life Insurance annuity and $28,000 from the trust. She still controlled the $130,000 brokerage account that she had opened with Josephine's money as well. But when she and her husband made a claim for the $167,000 death benefit under the Principal Mutual annuity, the insurance company launched an investigation that delayed payment.

Carl Fergo, the executor of Josephine's estate, also filed a lawsuit against Dietrick and PSA. During the course of the lawsuit, Dietrick tried to hide the existence of both the Principal Mutual annuity and the PSA brokerage account, but the litigation ultimately uncovered them. The Maryland Securities Commission launched an investigation, and in 2003, Dietrick consented to a settlement without admitting or denying the allegations. She was permanently barred from acting as a stockbroker or an RIA representative in that state.

Josephine's story is not unusual. Unethical brokers often take advantage of senior citizens, who are among the low-hanging fruit of the investment world, ripe for the picking by any broker or RIA. Brokerage firms try to prevent this by adopting rules that prohibit brokers from borrowing money from customers, accepting gifts above a nominal value, and holding a power of attorney. But supervisors are busy and sometimes miss violations, especially when the broker is producing large commissions.

Brokers know that the elderly—especially the widowed—often lack someone who will pay attention to them, listen to them, and make them feel important. Taking advantage of this fact, some brokers talk their way into a role in a senior citizen's life that gives them unfettered control over the senior citizen's financial affairs. The statistics tell the tale: While people age 60 and above make up 15 percent of the population, they account for 30 percent of fraud victims.

Protecting Your Parents

Dr. Robert Rousch of Baylor University Medical School does research to aid physicians who treat the elderly. He reports that 35 percent of people above 71 years old suffer from a condition known as mild cognitive impairment (MCI). People who suffer from MCI are four times more likely to fall victim to financial fraud. The Mayo Clinic defines MCI as "an intermediate stage between the expected cognitive decline of normal aging and the more pronounced decline of dementia." Symptoms include impulsiveness and poor judgment. There are 25 million Americans who are 71 or older. When you do the math, it shows that nearly 9 million elderly Americans take impulsiveness and poor judgment into their meetings with stockbrokers. Use your imagination and consider what an unethical broker can do with that.

Often, the adult children of seniors try talking to their parents about brokers who insinuate themselves into the seniors' lives. The children try to warn their parents, only to be rebuffed. You can imagine why elderly parents reject those warnings. The thought that they are not only lonely, but also vulnerable—that they have given their trust to someone who will take advantage of it—is painful. This is especially true of an elderly widow; the thought that one of the few people who seems to take a real interest in her life is doing so for ulterior motives is so devastating that she will not consider it to be within the realm of possibility. The most tragic cases I review are those of the adult children of elderly parents who are being controlled by unethical brokers. The senior citizens are unwilling to believe it and often refuse to consent to legal action against "their friend," so the abuse continues.

When confronted with an elderly relative who is unwilling to take action against a broker who has undue influence over that relative, the vigilant investor attacks the problem from the other end. Write to both the broker's manager and the firm's compliance department, with a copy to FINRA Enforcement, detailing the undue influence. If the senior cannot be convinced to terminate the relationship, you can at least shine some light on it for the firm and for FINRA, both of which can do something about it.

Abuse of elderly investors hurts not just the elderly customers, but also those to whom they would, without the broker's influence, leave their estate. Brokers can seriously frustrate the intentions of senior citizens who have saved for decades to leave a financial legacy for the next generation. A broker with a money motive may, as you read this, be drawing close to an elderly loved one of yours with plans to replace you in his will.

What can you do to protect elderly parents? First, make sure that your parents' doctor is performing a cognitive assessment at every checkup. You need to know if either of your parents suffers from MCI. Some assessments take as little as three minutes to perform and can accurately predict whether your parents are among the millions who are most vulnerable. Next, have a frank conversation with your parents about the dangers. I know, I know. The thought of having a conversation about this makes you uncomfortable, doesn't it? In a way, it feels like rubbing the salt of vulnerability into the wound of old age, like inflicting a gratuitous injury on someone who might otherwise be thinking about more pleasant things. But while inoculations always hurt for a second and might cause tenderness for a couple of days, the brief pain may save you from possible catastrophe.

A Template for Your Conversation

Given everything you've learned in this book, who or what can possibly prevent unethical brokers and RIAs from picking the low-hanging fruit of elderly investors? The vigilant investor. You can prevent a tragedy that would otherwise rob your parents of their sense of well-being.

Through more than two decades of protecting investors, I have developed a template for beginning the "money conversation" with parents. Talk to your siblings about this conversation in advance, and have all of them attend, if possible. Keep the tone upbeat. Acknowledge that your parents are still smart and competent, but remind them that there is safety in numbers, especially when the enemy is so numerous and so crafty. Make it clear that you don't want to take over; you want to help. Make any modifications to this template that you believe would help your parents take this information on board, but do not water down the essentials. Where you go next depends on how your parents respond. All you are trying to do with this first conversation is start a dialogue.

> Mom and/or Dad, if you thought someone was giving me bad advice or trying to take advantage of me, would you tell me—even if you thought it would make me feel bad? Why? Thank you. I'm glad to hear you say that. Can I have permission to do the same for you?
>
> I've been reading lately about all the investment scams out there and stockbrokers who take advantage of elderly customers. You wouldn't believe how often smart folks—especially those who are widowed—are victimized by stockbrokers and even by registered investment advisers. There are lots of cases of brokers taking over accounts that are owned by older people and draining them. I don't want you to think I'm trying to get my hands on your savings, but I love you enough to take that risk. I know that you didn't work and save for decades only to give everything to a brokerage firm or an investment adviser. Would you mind if I have someone investigate the broker you're using and perhaps take a look at your investments to make sure that they're suitable for someone your age?
>
> No one, no matter how smart, ever sees these people coming. Even big pension funds fall victim to these scams—and they're very wealthy and financially sophisticated. If it can happen to them, it can happen to anyone, including you and me, and I don't want to see it happen to you.

What is the worst that could happen? If your parent rebuffs you, is offended, or accuses you of being greedy, at least you've tried.

Maybe some of it got through and she will be more careful. And remember, you do not need your parent's permission to investigate her broker. All you need is a name. If the investigation reveals that the broker has a long rap sheet, you have hard evidence to present to your parent. If the broker has no record, it does not mean that he never will. You will at least know more about the broker than you did before, and you can better keep an eye on him. Have the conversation. There was a time when your parents protected you. Return the favor.

If your parents receive the conversation well, follow up by asking a few questions. Has your parents' broker ever asked to borrow money for any reason? Have your parents given the broker any gifts? Has the broker mentioned getting a power of attorney?

Next, review any paperwork from the broker or the RIA. Look at the account statements. Is there frequent trading? Are there unsuitably risky investments in large concentrations? Are there unexplained withdrawals? Is there a happiness letter (see Chapter 8) in your parents' paperwork? If so, use the tools we've discussed to find out all you can about this individual. If your review yields suspicious information, have the account reviewed by an experienced securities attorney. You can find one near you at www.piaba.org.

Please tell us about your conversation with your parents at www.investorswatchdog.com/contact/. We'll compile the stories—without revealing your identity—about how elderly parents react to the conversation on our site, and we'll share tips and tactics for making the conversations go more smoothly. Together, we can protect tens of thousands of elderly investors who might otherwise be picked clean by brokers and scam artists looking for low-hanging fruit. If we don't act, elderly people who may have been set to spend their final days in relatively comfortable retirement will instead spend those days in a Medicaid nursing home or living with you. Do not let this happen to those you love.

Not *My* Broker!

You and your parents might read stories like Josephine Fergo's and think, "Thank God my broker isn't like that." Don't be so sure. As we discussed in Chapter 1, every healthy human responds to these stories with an initial rejection of the idea that she could suffer the same fate. It is the optimism bias at work. Defeating that bias begins with recognizing it. You can then move past it to a vigilant investigation.

One other thing stands in the way, though: charisma. People describing conversations with skilled politicians relate how, even in a room crowded with people vying for their attention, they make you feel as if you are the only person in the room. You walk away convinced that they are "the real deal." All successful brokers have at least a little bit of that gift. The securities industry weeds out those who don't have it. All of the unethical brokers we've discussed in this book have it. So does your broker.

To properly evaluate any broker, you must realize that the broker's charisma—the ability to talk to people, to grab their trust without having done anything to earn it—is a natural trait, just like having red hair. The vigilant investor knows that charisma is no predictor of character. Giving a broker your trust based on his charisma, without a thorough investigation, makes as much sense as entrusting your nest egg to the next redheaded stockbroker you find.

The Deathbed Trader

In 2000, stockbroker Jimmie Griffith worked for McLaughlin, Vogel Securities Inc. (MVS) in California. One of his clients was JS (the customer's name does not appear in public records), a 76-year-old retired researcher for the University of California Davis. JS suffered from Parkinson's disease. He had a minor stroke in June 2000. Two months later, he was admitted to the hospital for surgery. After a short stay in a nursing home to recover from surgery, he returned home. On November 1, 2000, he was readmitted to the hospital, where he died on November 3, 2000.

Having buried her husband, JS's widow opened her next monthly statement from MVS to find that Griffith had sold JS's $100,000 position in the Putnam New Century Growth Fund on November 9, 2000, six days after his death. At an NASD disciplinary proceeding, Griffith claimed that JS had given him permission for the sale weeks earlier. The NASD panel didn't believe Griffith, suspended him from the securities industry for three months, and fined him $10,000 for unauthorized trades. As of this writing, Griffith is selling annuities and other insurance products.

In 2002, Adam Lazarus was a broker for Morgan Stanley in the Madison Avenue office in New York, assigned to handle the account of SD, a 92-year-old widow who was in failing health. A New York Stock Exchange (NYSE) disciplinary panel found that Lazarus had placed 31 unauthorized trades in SD's account, including several after her November 2003 death.

In December 2003, another of Lazarus's customers, BP, a former salesman at a department store, was admitted to the hospital for quadruple bypass surgery. During that hospitalization, Lazarus entered five unauthorized trades in BP's account. In September 2007, Lazarus consented, without admitting or denying the NYSE's allegations, to a 30-month bar from the securities industry for making improper trades in the accounts of sick and elderly customers.

As these stories illustrate, the abuse of senior investors goes beyond gifts, loans, and changing beneficiaries. Brokers know that a customer who is in declining health is unlikely to notice unauthorized trades. Proving unauthorized trading can be easier in these circumstances because a person who is approaching the end of her life rarely places securities trades from her deathbed. If you find a trade on a day that you know your loved one was unable to place it, you've uncovered unauthorized trading. Document it at once in writing to the branch manager and to FINRA.

If you are the beneficiary of a will and you receive investments as part of the estate, investigate to determine whether the estate is smaller because of misconduct by the broker. If you learn that the broker engaged in unauthorized trading or churning, or if he sold your 80-year-old mother a variable annuity, write a letter to the firm, with a copy to FINRA, detailing the misconduct so that future investors can avoid abuse at the hands of that broker.

A thorough review of a loved one's brokerage account can do more than reveal unethical behavior. It can reveal a broker who is worth keeping. Such a review is an unusually good opportunity to evaluate a broker based not on the broker's promises or charisma, but on how she treated a real customer, your deceased loved one—an evaluation that is measured not by the return (the market is responsible for that), but by whether the investments in the account were suitable for someone with your loved one's investment objectives and risk tolerance.

The League of Vigilant Investors

Imagine yourself in a long single-file line. The line is made up of all the people who will consider buying into what they don't yet realize is a very well-disguised investment scam run by people with enough charisma to talk a kid out of his Xbox 360. Like everyone else in the line, you are holding a bag of money representing your life savings.

The line is moving slowly toward a door. On the other side of that door is a 100-foot drop to a canyon floor strewn with the bodies of those who've stepped through the door already. No one in line can see the pile of bodies, hear the screams of those who step through, or perceive the drop until it is too late. Those who don't discover the fraud by the time they reach the front of the line step through the door and fall all the way to the bottom, where the architects of the scam take the bags of money, leaving their victims to suffer.

Eventually, one of the victims might crawl away from the pile and report the situation to regulators. The regulators will work quickly, but the investigation takes time and must follow certain procedures. Investors continue to fall, and there is nothing the regulators can do for those who lie broken on the pile. The regulators will track down the crooks and interview them, if they haven't already fled the country. Working as quickly as they can, the regulators climb up the canyon wall and lock the door. Then they set about bringing the architects of the scam to justice. They'll find as much of the money as they can. But most of it will have been spent beyond recovery.

Now imagine that as you stand in that line, you are equipped with the investigative tools and resources described in this book. Imagine also that, unlike most of the people in the line, you understand the cognitive biases that make it so difficult to find and pay attention to the evidence. Using these tools, you learn about the drop before you reach the front of the line. You have two choices. You can step out of line, carry your money away, and leave the others in the line to their fate. Or, you can become the best of what a vigilant investor can be. You can step out of line, run to the door, block the path, and call the regulators to begin their investigation before more people fall through. Every moment that you delay, another Josephine Fergo, another senior citizen, another baby boomer, another pension fund, another university endowment, or another elderly parent steps through the door.

We began this book with the story of a gang of vigilante senior citizens who banded together to try to recover what they had lost. They ended up in prison. But their story illustrates the power of what senior citizens can do when they come together with a mission. What if senior citizens were to unite before they entrusted their nest eggs to anyone?

Every day, 10,000 baby boomers turn 65, and 10,000 will turn 65 every day until 2030. Many of them will retire shortly after reaching 65 and will have to decide what to do with their 401(k) balances. Scams and unethical brokers await them. Millions of retiring boomers will consider financial advisers and investments that promise growth and safety, but produce only financial ruin. Do you hope that those who've become vigilant investors step away silently when they uncover danger? Or do you hope that they make some noise?

Empowered, retired baby boomers can be the solution to the epidemic of investment fraud that if left unchecked will cost investors nearly $1 trillion in the 19 years that it will take the last baby boomer to reach 65. I propose that retiring seniors band together to form associations of vigilant investors (AVIs) that are committed to practicing the disciplined due diligence methods in this book, to alerting regulators, and to warning others when they discover danger.

Vigilant due diligence requires legwork. What if an association of vigilant investors in Seattle needs a state courthouse records search in Dade County, Florida? Call the Miami AVI. What if the AVI in Boston needs to walk into the offices of a supposed hedge fund auditor in Century City, California? Call the AVI in Los Angeles. Perhaps AARP or other organizations representing seniors can help organize these groups. Start in your backyard and ask the local AARP chapter to help.

There is only so much golf you can play, right? Your parents' generation needs you. Those to whom you hope to leave a financial legacy need you. We all need you to step forward and become a force that reshapes the investing landscape in a way that no Congress, no regulator, and no prosecutor ever can. You are holding the playbook.

Due Diligence for the Vigilant

The vigilant investor:

▶ Reports suspected cases of undue influence by brokers in writing to the broker's manager, the firm's compliance department, and FINRA Enforcement

▶ Makes sure that his parents' doctor performs a cognitive assessment at every checkup

▶ Has a frank conversation with her parents about the dangers of fraud and unethical brokers, and asks permission to help

▶ Investigates his parents' broker

▶ Knows that charisma is no predictor of character and investigates her parents' broker even if her parents will not

▶ Looks for unauthorized trading and other violations in the accounts of loved ones who are hospitalized or recently deceased

▶ Uses the tools and tactics in this book to protect not just himself, but the rest of the investing public

▶ Knows that, with other vigilant investors, she can cleanse the investing landscape in a way that no Congress, no regulator, and no prosecutor ever can

Notes

Chapter 1

1. In the parlance of scams and swindles, the victim or prospective victim is called the "mark."
2. C. S. Lewis, *Mere Christianity* (Orem, Utah: Granite Publishers, 2006).
3. W. A. Clouston, ed., *Book of Wise Sayings* (Minneapolis, Minn.: Fili-Quarian Classics, 2010).
4. Stephen Greenspan, *The Annals of Gullibility: Why We Get Duped and How to Avoid It* (Westport, Conn.: Praeger, 2008).
5. Kristen J. Prentice, James M. Gold, and William T. Carpenter, Jr., "Optimistic Bias in the Perception of Personal Risk: Patterns in Schizophrenia," *American Journal of Psychiatry*, 162, no. 3 (2005), pp. 507–512.
6. Jonah Lehrer, *How We Decide* (Boston: Houghton Mifflin Harcourt, 2009).

Chapter 2

1. The Commodities Futures Trading Commission (CFTC) also handles investment fraud cases if they involve investments within the commission's jurisdiction: currency trading, oil futures, commodities pools, and other such areas.
2. There are also enforcement accountants on the SEC's enforcement team.
3. A disgorgement is designed to deprive the violator of the proceeds of the fraud. Disgorgement payments often go to the U.S. Treasury rather than to defrauded victims.
4. The author has been appointed receiver in three SEC enforcement cases and two Federal Trade Commission cases.
5. The most sweeping overhaul of financial regulation since the 1930s, the Dodd-Frank Act addresses everything from derivatives trading to the duty that stockbrokers owe their customers. It aims to end the practices and abuses that led to the financial crisis of 2007 and prevent a recurrence of the conditions that led to that crisis. The act closes loopholes that allowed many investment advisers to avoid registration and requires hedge funds bigger than $150 million to register with the SEC and maintain certain records. Dodd-Frank also creates two new regulators: The Consumer Financial Protection Bureau will monitor predatory lending and abuses by credit card companies and banks, and the Financial Stability Oversight Council will identify and respond to emerging risks through the financial system.
6. This is the latest period for which full statistics are available.
7. As Eliot Spitzer demonstrated in the late 1990s and early 2000s, state attorneys general can also enforce investment laws. Spitzer revealed corruption at the biggest

firms on Wall Street, and his successor as New York attorney general has taken up the mantle.

8. This is a much higher bar to clear than the preponderance of the evidence (more likely than not), which is standard in civil cases.

9. Civil contempt is designed to motivate the defendant to comply with a previous order by putting him in jail until he complies. While he was in jail, Hatfield devised a payment plan for paying a small amount of the disgorgement ordered in the Marada case. That plan was enough to convince the court that Hatfield had learned his lesson and that the imprisonment for civil contempt had done its job.

10. Experts report that 1 in every 25 people is a sociopath.

11. Athletes are so often the target of con artists that the NFLPA tries to weed out the likely frauds and recommend only reputable financial advisers.

12. The vast majority of scam artists are men.

13. One such site is http://finance.yahoo.com/q/hp?s=A+Historical+Prices.

14. You can find that number at http://www.sec.gov/contact/addresses.htm.

15. The expenses will always be an estimate. At IW, we call the landlord for the adviser's building and find out the cost per square foot of space in the building and how much square footage is on each floor. We visit the office, sometimes posing as a prospective client. You can estimate the payroll expenses by searching on résumé sites for jobs in the area. An administrative assistant in New York will make more than someone in the same position in Omaha. The ADV will give you a range for how many employees work at the firm and tell you how many of them give investment advice.

16. Certified Financial Planner, a designation given by the Certified Financial Planning Board of Standards (CFP board) after extensive training and successful passage of an examination. Holders of the CFP designation agree to comply with an ethical code that is more stringent than that required by law.

17. Chartered Financial Analyst. The CFA Institute awards the designation to candidates who pass three levels of examination covering accounting, economics, ethics, money management, and security analysis.

18. If you uncover an adviser who is trying to mislead investors this way, please call Investor's Watchdog at 1-877-423-WDOG and report it, or send us the information via e-mail to pat@investorswatchdog.com. We will add that information to our database, where it can help protect other investors.

19. If you cannot get a year's worth of statements, get as many as you can. You will be able to extrapolate from the figures calculated from those few statements.

20. Every trade costs money.

21. Fee-only advisers will ask you to write them a check for their time and advice, which is appropriate, but never for an investment.

22. Please send the information to Investor's Watchdog so that we can protect others from this Thief.

23. Registered investment advisers are supposed to list outside businesses on their ADV. However, the vigilant investor looks further.

Chapter 3

1. The National Council of Churches, the Chicago Housing Authority's pension fund, and even the South Pacific nation of Nauru have all fallen victim to prime bank scams.
2. Laundering money through numerous bank accounts in several countries makes it harder to trace and harder to recover.
3. The short con, by contrast, aims to relieve the mark of whatever she has on her at the time—think three-card monte.
4. Like mutual funds, hedge funds pool investors' money and invest those funds in financial instruments in an effort to make a positive return. Many hedge funds seek to profit in all kinds of markets by using leveraging and other speculative investment practices that may increase the risk of investment loss.
5. Marquez, a former aide to billionaire George Soros, left Bayou in 2001.
6. Luckily, the Arizona securities commissioner's office, which had been watching the prime bank scamster, succeeded in freezing that money before the scamster could take it.
7. Judge McMahon also sentenced Marino to 20 years in prison. She sentenced Marquez, who had left Bayou before the scam reached the $100 million mark, to 51 months in prison.
8. There is no parole in the federal criminal justice system, but inmates can earn credit toward their time served for good behavior.
9. From the David Mamet play and movie *Glengarry Glen Ross*, in which the salesmen compete for access to leads to the marks who are most likely to buy.

Chapter 4

1. U.S. investors have no difficulty buying shares on the Toronto Exchange, just as Canadian investors can buy U.S. stocks in U.S. markets.
2. Canadian dollars.
3. Bankruptcy, receivership, departure of certain officers or directors, discovery that previously issued financial statements are inaccurate, and other such events trigger the requirement that the company file an 8-K.
4. A successful due diligence investigator must be as bold as a scam artist. Investors who cannot see themselves undertaking this level of hands-on investigation must either hire an experienced investigator to do it for them or avoid the investment. Bypassing this level of investigation and hoping for the best is often a very expensive mistake.
5. Fastow pleaded guilty to conspiracy as part of a plea bargain that required him to cooperate with the government's prosecution of Skilling and Lay. He was sentenced to 10 years in prison. A federal jury convicted Skilling on 19 counts of securities and wire fraud. He received a prison sentence of 24 years and 4 months. The jury convicted Lay on six counts of securities and wire fraud. On July 5, 2006, while awaiting sentencing, Lay died. Arthur Andersen was convicted of obstructing jus-

tice by shredding documents and deleting e-mails as the FBI closed in. Its conviction was overturned by an appellate court because of a faulty jury instruction. However, the firm had gone out of business by that time.

Chapter 7

1. The correct industry term for a stockbroker is *registered representative*.
2. Oppenheimer Holdings, Inc. (the parent company), has 94 offices in 82 cities, including Buenos Aires, Caracas, Hong Kong, London, and Tel Aviv, and an investment management arm that manages $16.2 billion. Its gross revenue in 2009 was $991 million.
3. http://www.sec.state.ma.us/sct/sctopp/consentorder.pdf.
4. Formerly known as the National Association of Securities Dealers, Inc. (NASD), FINRA is the self-regulatory organization to which the SEC has delegated authority to oversee the brokerage industry. FINRA has its own enforcement staff, which investigates suspected violations and takes disciplinary action against offenders. Like all securities regulators, it is far too small and underfunded for the task that confronts it. While a detour into the details of FINRA rules is beyond the scope of this book, interested investors can find those rules at www.finra.org/Industry/Regulation/FINRARules/.
5. File a complaint online at www.finra.org/Investors/ProtectYourself/ or call FINRA at (301) 590-6500.

Chapter 8

1. In 2008, Wells Fargo acquired Wachovia. AGE was folded into Wells Fargo Investments.

Chapter 9

1. Because FINRA used to be known as the NASD, you should use "NASD" as a search term as well.
2. Unit investment trusts (UITs) are similar to mutual funds, but they don't actively trade the portfolio. UITs buy a relatively fixed portfolio of securities and hold them with little or no change until the fixed termination date of the UIT, at which time the trust sells the portfolio and pays the proceeds to the owners of the UIT.

Chapter 11

1. Angela A. Hung, Noreen Clancy, Jeff Dominitz, et al., *Investor and Industry Perspectives on Investment Advisers and Broker-Dealers* (Santa Monica, Calif.: RAND Institute for Civil Justice, 2008).
2. Because Freese managed less than $25 million, he was registered through his state securities regulator, rather than through the SEC. Under the Dodd-Frank Act, the threshold for SEC registration is now $100 million. RIAs who manage less than that amount will register through, and be examined by, state regulators.

Index